Elegant 2-PIECE SETS
in thread crochet

Kathryn A. Clark is one of those admirable persons who does well at everything she tries. And when you know a little more about her, it's easy to spot the reason for Kathryn's adeptness at crochet. It's in her genes.

"When I wanted a crocheted vest, my mother sat down with me and we learned to crochet together," says Kathryn. "And then my mother went on to learn all kinds of additional art and craft skills. My father worked as an accountant until his retirement, then went on to do finish work for a builder. All of my five siblings pursued their own artistic endeavors."

Years after Kathryn's first crochet lesson, she learned that her great-grandmother, whom she never met, was also an avid crocheter.

To achieve success as a designer, Kathryn coupled her love of crochet with the discipline to develop patterns. Her exquisite designs reflect her father's skill in mathematics and her mother's practicality.

Says Kathryn, "Even though you can buy a finished product in a store or perhaps hire someone to create it for you, there is enjoyment and a feeling of satisfaction in accomplishing something for yourself."

Clothing this exquisite can only be handmade. That's why boutiques charge an exorbitant price for similar garments. However, you can avoid sticker shock by taking fashion matters into your own two hands. Under your skillful fingers, a crochet hook can transform simple cotton thread into this wardrobe of sophisticated separates. The two-piece skirt sets by Kathryn A. Clark will reward you time and again as you pair the pieces with other tops, pants, and skirts. Even better, these all-original designs won't be found in stores anywhere—and that can't be said of their pricey cousins at the mall!

LEISURE ARTS, INC.
Little Rock, Arkansas

Contents

Midnight in the garden

The romance of a flower-scented evening is yours to enjoy anytime with this dramatic skirt set. Horizontal stripes create the illusion of gathered tiers on the full skirt, which hangs gracefully from a drawstring waist. The double-breasted jacket is elegant with an asymmetrical hem and bell sleeves. Search your closet for separates that will complement these petal-perfect pieces.

jacket

◀▦▦▦▭ INTERMEDIATE

FINISHED CHEST SIZE:

X-Small: 29" (73.5 cm)   Large: 41^1/$_2$" (105.5 cm)
Small: 33" (84 cm)   X-Large: 46^1/$_2$" (118 cm)
Medium: 36^3/$_4$" (93.5 cm)

Instructions are written with sizes X-Small and Small in the first set of braces { } and with sizes Medium, Large, and X-Large in the second set of braces. Instructions will be easier to read if you circle all the numbers pertaining to your size. If only one number is given, it applies to all sizes.

MATERIALS

Bedspread Weight Cotton Thread
(size 10)
   [350 yards (320 meters) per ball]:
   Black - {7-7}{8-9-10} balls
   Red - 1 ball
   Yellow - 1 ball
Steel crochet hook, size 7 (1.65 mm)
   or size needed for gauge
^{5}/$_8$" (16 mm) buttons: 4
Sewing needle and matching thread

GAUGE:

In pattern:
   (5 dc in next st, sc in next st)
   4 times = 3^7/$_8$" (10 cm);
   12 rows = 3" (7.5 cm)

SPECIAL STITCHES:

Hdc in top of dc just made: YO, insert hook through one horizontal bar and one vertical bar of specified stitch *(Fig. 5, page 95)*, YO, pull up a loop, YO, pull through all loops on hook.

Tr: YO twice, insert hook in st or sp indicated, YO and pull up a loop, (YO and draw through 2 loops on hook) 3 times.

BACK
With Black, ch {122-138} {154-170-186}.

Row 1 (right side):
Sc in second ch from hook, * sk next 3 chs, 5 dc in next ch, sk next 3 chs, sc in next ch, rep from * across: {15-17}{19-21-23} 5-dc groups.

NOTE: Loop a short piece of thread around any stitch to mark Row 1 as **right** side.

Row 2:
Ch 3 (**counts as first dc, now and throughout**), turn; 2 dc in same st, sk next 2 dc, sc in next dc, (sk next 2 dc, 5 dc in next sc, sk next 2 dc, sc in next dc) {14-16}{18-20-22} times, sk next 2 dc, 3 dc in last sc: {14-16}{18-20-22} 5-dc groups and 2 3-dc groups.

Row 3:
Ch 1, turn; sc in first st, * sk next 2 dc, 5 dc in next sc, sk next 2 dc, sc in next dc, rep from * across.

Rows 3a and 3b:
Medium, Large, and X-Large Only:
Rep Rows 2 and 3.

Row 4:
Ch 3, turn; 3 dc in same st, sk next 2 dc, sc in next dc, (sk next 2 dc, 5 dc in next sc, sk next 2 dc, sc in next dc) {14-16}{18-20-22} times, sk next 2 dc, 4 dc in last sc: {14-16}{18-20-22} 5-dc groups and 2 4-dc groups.

Row 5:
Ch 3, turn; sc in next dc, (sk next 2 dc, 5 dc in next sc, sk next 2 dc, sc in next dc) {15-17}{19-21-23} times, dc in last dc.

Row 6:
Turn; sk first dc, (hdc, 4 dc) in next sc, sk next 2 dc, sc in next dc, (sk next 2 dc, 5 dc in next sc, sk next 2 dc, sc in next dc) {14-16}{18-20-22} times, sk next 2 dc, (4 dc, hdc) in next sc, sl st in last dc.

Row 7:
Turn; sl st in first hdc, ch 4 (**counts as first tr, now and throughout**), 2 dc in same st, sk next dc, sc in next dc, (sk next 2 dc, 5 dc in next sc, sk next 2 dc, sc in next dc) {15-17} {19-21-23} times, sk next dc, (2 dc, tr) in last hdc.

Row 8:
Ch 1, turn; sc in first st, * sk next 2 dc, 5 dc in next sc, sk next 2 dc, sc in next st, rep from * across: {16-18}{20-22-24} 5-dc groups.

Row 9:
Ch 3, turn; 2 dc in same st, sk next 2 dc, sc in next dc, (sk next 2 dc, 5 dc in next sc, sk next 2 dc, sc in next dc) {15-17}{19-21-23} times, sk next 2 dc, 3 dc in last sc.

Row 10:
Rep Row 8.

Row 11:
Ch 3, turn; 3 dc in same st, sk next 2 dc, sc in next dc, (sk next 2 dc, 5 dc in next sc, sk next 2 dc, sc in next dc) {15-17}{19-21-23} times, sk next 2 dc, 4 dc in last sc: {15-17}{19-21-23} 5-dc groups and 2 4-dc groups.

Row 12:
Ch 3, turn; sc in next st, (sk next 2 dc, 5 dc in next sc, sk next 2 dc, sc in next dc) {16-18}{20-22-24} times, dc in last dc.

Row 13:
Turn; sk first dc, (hdc, 4 dc) in next sc, sk next 2 dc, sc in next dc, (sk next 2 dc, 5 dc in next sc, sk next 2 dc, sc in next dc) {15-17}{19-21-23} times, sk next 2 dc, (4 dc, hdc) in next sc, sl st in last dc.

Row 14:
Turn; sl st in first hdc, ch 4, 2 dc in same st, sk next dc, sc in next dc, (sk next 2 dc, 5 dc in next sc, sk next 2 dc, sc in next dc) {16-18}{20-22-24} times, sk next dc, (2 dc, tr) in last hdc.

Row 15:
Ch 1, turn; sc in first st, * sk next 2 dc, 5 dc in next sc, sk next 2 dc, sc in next st, rep from * across: {17-19}{21-23-25} 5-dc groups.

Row 16:
Ch 3, turn; 2 dc in same st, sk next 2 dc, sc in next dc, (sk next 2 dc, 5 dc in next sc, sk next 2 dc, sc in next dc) {16-18}{20-22-24} times, sk next 2 dc, 3 dc in last sc.

Row 17:
Rep Row 15.

Row 18:
Ch 3, turn; 3 dc in same st, sk next 2 dc, sc in next dc, (sk next 2 dc, 5 dc in next sc, sk next 2 dc, sc in next dc) {16-18}{20-22-24} times, sk next 2 dc, 4 dc in last sc: {16-18}{20-22-24} 5-dc groups and 2 4-dc groups.

Row 19:
Ch 3, turn; sc in next dc, (sk next 2 dc, 5 dc in next sc, sk next 2 dc, sc in next dc) {17-19}{21-23-25} times, dc in last dc.

Row 20:
Turn; sk first dc, (hdc, 4 dc) in next sc, sk next 2 dc, sc in next dc, (sk next 2 dc, 5 dc in next sc, sk next 2 dc, sc in next dc) {16-18}{20-22-24} times, sk next 2 dc, (4 dc, hdc) in next sc, sl st in last dc.

Row 21:
Turn; sl st in first hdc, ch 4, 2 dc in same st, sk next dc, sc in next dc, (sk next 2 dc, 5 dc in next sc, sk next 2 dc, sc in next dc) {17-19} {21-23-25} times, sk next dc, (2 dc, tr) in last hdc.

Row 22:
Ch 1, turn; sc in first st, * sk next 2 dc, 5 dc in next sc, sk next 2 dc, sc in next st, rep from * across: {18-20} {22-24-26} 5-dc groups.

Row 23:
Ch 3, turn; 2 dc in same st, sk next 2 dc, sc in next dc, (sk next 2 dc, 5 dc in next sc, sk next 2 dc, sc in next dc) {17-19}{21-23-25} times, sk next 2 dc, 3 dc in last sc.

Rows 24 and 25:
Rep Rows 22 and 23.

X-Small Only:
Row 26:
Rep Row 22. Fasten off.

Small, Medium, Large, and X-Large Only:
Row 26:
Ch 1, turn; sc in first st, sk next 2 dc, (dc, 2 hdc, dc) in next sc, sk next 2 dc, sc in next dc, (sk next 2 dc, 5 dc in next sc, sk next 2 dc, sc in next dc) {20}{22-24-26} times, sk next 2 dc, (dc, 2 hdc, dc) in next sc, sk next 2 dc, sc in next dc. Fasten off.

Row 27:
With **right** side facing, join Black with sc in third dc of first 5-dc group *(see Joining with Sc, page 95)*, (sk next 2 dc, 5 dc in next sc, sk next 2 dc, sc in next dc) {17-19}{21-23-25} times.

Row 28:
Turn; sl st in first 4 sts, ch 1, sc in same st, (sk next 2 dc, 5 dc in next sc, sk next 2 dc, sc in next dc) {16-16}{18-20-22} times.

X-Small, Small, and Medium Only:
Row 29:
Ch 3, turn; 2 dc in same st, sk next 2 dc, sc in next dc, (sk next 2 dc, 5 dc in next sc, sk next 2 dc, sc in next dc) {15-15}{17} times, sk next 2 dc, 3 dc in last sc.

Row 30:
Ch 1, turn; sc in first st, (sk next 2 dc, 5 dc in next sc, sk next 2 dc, sc in next dc) {16-16}{18} times.

Rows 31-59:
Rep Rows 29 and 30, 14 times, then rep Row 29 once **more**.

Row 60:
Ch 1, turn; sc in first st, † sk next 2 dc, (dc, 2 hdc, dc) in next sc, sk next 2 dc, sc in next dc †, rep from † to † {3-4}{4} times **more**, mark last sc made for end of right shoulder, rep from † to † 8 times, mark last sc made for beg of left shoulder, rep from † to † {4-4}{5} times. Fasten off.

Skip to Right Front.

Large and X-Large Only:
Row 29:
Ch 3, turn; dc in same st, sk next 2 dc, sc in next dc, (sk next 2 dc, 5 dc in next sc, sk next 2 dc, sc in next dc) {19-21} times, sk next 2 dc, 2 dc in last sc.

Row 30:
Turn; sk first 2 dc, (hdc, 3 dc) in next sc, sk next 2 dc, sc in next dc, (sk next 2 dc, 5 dc in next sc, sk next 2 dc, sc in next dc) {18-20} times, sk next 2 dc, (3 dc, hdc) in next sc, sk next dc, sl st in last dc.

Row 31:
Turn; sl st in first hdc, ch 1, sc in next st, (sk next 2 dc, 5 dc in next sc, sk next 2 dc, sc in next dc) {19-21} times, leave last hdc unworked.

Row 32:
Ch 3, turn; dc in same st, sk next 2 dc, sc in next dc, (sk next 2 dc, 5 dc in next sc, sk next 2 dc, sc in next dc) {18-20} times, sk next 2 dc, 2 dc in last sc.

Row 33:
Turn; sk first 2 dc, (hdc, 3 dc) in next sc, sk next 2 dc, sc in next dc, (sk next 2 dc, 5 dc in next sc, sk next 2 dc, sc in next dc) {17-19} times, sk next 2 dc, (3 dc, hdc) in next sc, sk next dc, sl st in last dc.

Row 34:
Turn; sl st in first hdc, ch 1, sc in next st, (sk next 2 dc, 5 dc in next sc, sk next 2 dc, sc in next dc) {18-20} times, leave last hdc unworked.

Row 35:
Ch 3, turn; 2 dc in first st, sk next 2 dc, sc in next dc, (sk next 2 dc, 5 dc in next sc, sk next 2 dc, sc in next dc) {17-19} times, sk next 2 dc, 3 dc in next sc.

Row 36:
Ch 1, turn; sc in first st, (sk next 2 dc, 5 dc in next sc, sk next 2 dc, sc in next dc) {18-20} times.

Rows 37 thru {61-63}:
Rep Rows 35 and 36, {12-13} times, then rep Row 35 once **more**.

Row {62-64}:
Ch 1, turn; sc in first st, † sk next 2 dc, (dc, 2 hdc, dc) in next sc, sk next 2 dc, sc in next dc †, rep from † to † 4 times **more**, mark last sc made for end of right shoulder, rep from † to †{8-10} times, mark last sc made for beg of left shoulder, rep from † to † 5 times. Fasten off.

RIGHT FRONT

With Black, ch {96-104} {112-128-144}.

Row 1 (right side):
2 Dc in fourth ch from hook, sk next 3 chs, sc in next ch, (sk next 3 chs, 5 dc in next ch, sk 3 chs, sc in next ch) {11-12}{13-15-17} times.

NOTE: Mark Row 1 as **right** side.

Row 2:
Ch 3, turn; 2 dc in same st, sk next 2 dc, sc in next dc, (sk next 2 dc, 5 dc in next sc, sk next 2 dc, sc in next dc) {11-12}{13-15-17} times.

Row 3 (Buttonhole Row):
Ch 3, turn; 2 dc in same st, sk next 2 dc, sc in next dc, (dc, ch 3, dc) in next sc, sk next 2 dc, sc in next dc, (sk next 2 dc, 5 dc in next sc, sk next 2 dc, sc in next dc) {5-5}{5-6-7} times, sk next 2 dc, (dc, ch 3, dc) in next sc, sk next 2 dc, sc in next dc, (sk next 2 dc, 5 dc in next sc, sk next 2 dc, sc in next dc) {4-5}{6-7-8} times.

Row 4:
X-Small and Small Only:
Ch 3, turn; 3 dc in same st, sk next 2 dc, sc in next dc, (sk next 2 dc, 5 dc in next sc, sk next 2 dc, sc in next dc) {3-4} times, † sk next 2 dc, 5 dc in next sc, sc in next ch-3 sp, 5 dc in next sc, sk next 2 dc, sc in next dc †, (sk next 2 dc, 5 dc in next sc, sk next 2 dc, sc in next dc) 4 times, rep from † to † once.

Medium, Large, and X-Large Only:
Ch 3, turn; 2 dc in same st, sk next 2 dc, sc in next dc, (sk next 2 dc, 5 dc in next sc, sk next 2 dc, sc in next dc) {5-6-7} times, † sk next 2 dc, 5 dc in next sc, sc in next ch-3 sp, 5 dc in next sc, sk next 2 dc, sc in next dc †, (sk next 2 dc, 5 dc in next sc, sk next 2 dc, sc in next dc) {4-5-6} times, rep from † to † once.

Row 5:
X-Small and Small Only:
Ch 3, turn; 2 dc in same st, sk next 2 dc, sc in next dc, (sk next 2 dc, 5 dc in next sc, sk next 2 dc, sc in next dc) {11-12} times, dc in last dc.

Medium, Large, and X-Large Only:
Ch 3, turn; 2 dc in same st, sk next 2 dc, sc in next dc, (sk next 2 dc, 5 dc in next sc, sk next 2 dc, sc in next dc) {13-15-17} times.

Row 5a:
Medium, Large, and X-Large Only:
Ch 3, turn; 3 dc in same st, sk next 2 dc, sc in next dc, (sk next 2 dc, 5 dc in next sc, sk next 2 dc, sc in next dc) {13-15-17} times.

Row 5b:
Medium, Large, and X-Large Only:
Ch 3, turn; 2 dc in same st, sk next 2 dc, sc in next dc, (sk next 2 dc, 5 dc in next sc, sk next 2 dc, sc in next dc) {13-15-17} times, dc in last dc.

Row 6:
Turn; sk first dc, (hdc, 4 dc) in next sc, sk next 2 dc, sc in next dc, * sk next 2 dc, 5 dc in next sc, sk next 2 dc, sc in next dc, rep from * across.

Row 7:
Ch 3, turn; 2 dc in same st, sk next 2 dc, sc in next dc, (sk next 2 dc, 5 dc in next sc, sk next 2 dc, sc in next dc) {11-12}{13-15-17} times, sk next dc, (2 dc, tr) in next hdc.

Row 8:
Ch 1, turn; sc in first st, * sk next 2 dc, 5 dc in next sc, sk next 2 dc, sc in next dc, rep from * across.

Row 9:
Ch 3, turn; 2 dc in same st, sk next 2 dc, sc in next dc, (sk next 2 dc, 5 dc in next sc, sk next 2 dc, sc in next dc) {11-12}{13-15-17} times, sk next 2 dc, 3 dc in last sc.

Row 10:
Rep Row 8.

Row 11:
Ch 3, turn; 2 dc in same st, sk next 2 dc, sc in next dc, (sk next 2 dc, 5 dc in next sc, sk next 2 dc, sc in next dc) {11-12}{13-15-17} times, sk next 2 dc, 4 dc in last sc.

Row 14:
Turn; sl st in first hdc, ch 4, 2 dc in same st, sk next dc, sc in next dc, (sk next 2 dc, 5 dc in next sc, sk next 2 dc, sc in next dc) {4-5}{6-7-8} times, † sk next 2 dc, 5 dc in next sc, sc in next ch-3 sp, skip next dc, 5 dc in next sc, sk next 2 dc, sc in next dc †, (sk next 2 dc, 5 dc in next sc, sk next 2 dc, sc in next dc) {4-4}{4-5-6} times, rep from † to † once.

Row 20:
Turn; sk first dc, (hdc, 4 dc) in next sc, sk next 2 dc, sc in next dc, * sk next 2 dc, 5 dc in next sc, sk next 2 dc, sc in next dc, rep from * across.

Row 21:
Ch 3, turn; 2 dc in same st, sk next 2 dc, sc in next dc, (sk next 2 dc, 5 dc in next sc, sk next 2 dc, sc in next dc) {12-13}{14-16-18} times, sk next dc, (2 dc, tr) in last hdc.

Row 12:
Ch 3, turn; sc in next st, (sk next 2 dc, 5 dc in next sc, sk next 2 dc, sc in next dc) {12-13}{14-16-18} times.

Row 13 (Buttonhole Row):
Ch 3, turn; 2 dc in same st, sk next 2 dc, sc in next dc, sk next 2 dc, (dc, ch 3, dc) in next sc, sk next 2 dc, sc in next dc, (sk next 2 dc, 5 dc in next sc, sk next 2 dc, sc in next dc) {5-5}{5-6-7} times, sk next 2 dc, (dc, ch 3, dc) in next sc, sk next 2 dc, sc in next dc, (sk next 2 dc, 5 dc in next sc, sk next 2 dc, sc in next dc) {4-5}{6-7-8} times, sk next 2 dc, (4 dc, hdc) in next sc, sl st in last dc.

Rows 15-17:
Ch 3; turn; 2 dc in first st, sk next 2 dc, sc in next dc, * sk next 2 dc, 5 dc in next sc, sk next 2 dc, sc in next st, rep from * across.

Row 18:
Ch, 3, turn; 3 dc in same st, sk next 2 dc, sc in next dc, * sk next 2 dc, 5 dc in next sc, sk next 2 dc, sc in next dc, rep from * across.

Row 19:
Ch 3, turn; 2 dc in same st, sk next 2 dc, sc in next dc, (sk next 2 dc, 5 dc in next sc, sk next 2 dc, sc in next dc) {12-13}{14-16-18} times, dc in last dc.

Row 22:
Ch 1, turn; sc in first st, * sk next 2 dc, 5 dc in next sc, sk next 2 dc, sc in next dc, rep from * across.

Row 23:
Ch 3, turn; 2 dc in same st, sk next 2 dc, sc in next dc, (sk next 2 dc, 5 dc in next sc, sk next 2 dc, sc in next dc) {12-13}{14-16-18} times, sk next 2 dc, 3 dc in last sc.

Rows 24 and 25:
Rep Rows 22 and 23.

X-Small Only:
Row 26:
Rep Row 22.

Small, Medium, Large, and X-Large Only:

Row 26:
Ch 1, turn; sc in first st, sk next 2 dc, (dc, 2 hdc, dc) in next sc, sk next 2 dc, sc in next dc, * sk next 2 dc, 5 dc in next sc, sk next 2 dc, sc in next dc, rep from * across.

Row 27:
Ch 3, turn; 2 dc in same st, sk next 2 dc, sc in next dc, (sk next 2 dc, 5 dc in next sc, sk next 2 dc, sc in next dc) {12-12}{13-15-17} times, leave remaining sts unworked.

Row 28:
Turn; skip first sc, sl st in next 2 dc, ch 1, sc in next dc, (sk next 2 dc, 5 dc in next sc, sk next 2 dc, sc in next dc) {12-12}{13-15-17} times.

Row 29:
X-Small, Small, and Medium Only:
Ch 3, turn; 2 dc in same st, sk next 2 dc, sc in next dc, (sk next 2 dc, 5 dc in next sc, sk next 2 dc, sc in next dc) {11-11}{12} times, sk next 2 dc, 3 dc in last sc.

Large and X-Large Only:
Ch 3, turn; 2 dc in same st, sk next 2 dc, sc in next dc, (sk next 2 dc, 5 dc in next sc, sk next 2 dc, sc in next dc) {14-16} times, sk next 2 dc, 2 dc in last sc.

Row 30:
X-Small, Small, and Medium Only:
Ch 1, turn; sc in first st, * sk next 2 dc, 5 dc in next sc, sk next 2 dc, sc in next dc, rep from * across.

Large and X-Large Only:
Turn; sk first 2 dc, (hdc, 3 dc) in next sc, sk next 2 dc, sc in next dc, (sk next 2 dc, 5 dc in next sc, sk next 2 dc, sc in next dc) {14-16} times.

Rows 31-42:
X-Small, Small, and Medium Only:
Rep Rows 29 and 30, 6 times; do **not** fasten off.

Skip to Right Lapel Shaping.

Large and X-Large Only:
Row 31:
Ch 3, turn; 2 dc in same st, sk next 2 dc, sc in next dc, (sk next 2 dc, 5 dc in next sc, sk next 2 dc, sc in next dc) {14-16} times, leave last hdc unworked.

Row 32:
Ch 3, turn; dc in same st, sk next 2 dc, sc in next dc, (sk next 2 dc, 5 dc in next sc, sk next 2 dc, sc in next dc) {14-16} times.

Row 33:
Ch 3, turn; 2 dc in same st, sk next 2 dc, sc in next dc, (sk next 2 dc, 5 dc in next sc, sk next 2 dc, sc in next dc) {13-15} times, sk next 2 dc, (3 dc, hdc) in next sc, sk next dc, sl st in last dc.

Row 34:
Turn; sl st in first hdc, ch 1, sc in next dc, (sk next 2 dc, 5 dc in next sc, sk next 2 dc, sc in next dc) {14-16} times.

Row 35:
Ch 3, turn; 2 dc in same st, sk next 2 dc, sc in next dc, (sk next 2 dc, 5 dc in next sc, sk next 2 dc, sc in next dc) {13-15} times, sk next 2 dc, 3 dc in last sc.

Row 36:
Ch 1, turn; sc in first st, * sk next 2 dc, 5 dc in next sc, sk next 2 dc, sc in next dc, rep from * across.

Rows 37 thru {42-44}:
Rep Rows 35 and 36, {3-4} times.

RIGHT LAPEL SHAPING
Row 1:
Ch 3, turn; sk next 2 dc, sc in next dc, (sk next 2 dc, 5 dc in next sc, sk next 2 dc, sc in next dc) {11-11}{12-13-15} times, sk next 2 dc, 3 dc in last sc.

Row 2:
Ch 1, turn; sc in first st, (sk next 2 dc, 5 dc in next sc, sk next 2 dc, sc in next dc) {11-11}{12-13-15} times, sk next 2 dc, dc in next sc, 2 dc in last dc.

Row 3:
Ch 1, turn; sc in first st, (sk next 2 dc, 5 dc in next sc, sk next 2 dc, sc in next dc) {11-11}{12-13-15} times, sk next 2 dc, 3 dc in last sc.

Row 4:
Ch 1, turn; sc in first st, (sk next 2 dc, 5 dc in next sc, sk next 2 dc, sc in next dc) {11-11}{12-13-15} times, sk next 2 dc, dc in last sc.

Row 5:
Ch 3, turn; dc in same st and in next sc, sk next 2 dc, sc in next dc, (sk next 2 dc, 5 dc in next sc, sk next 2 dc, sc in next dc) {10-10}{11-12-14} times, sk next 2 dc, 3 dc in last sc.

Row 6:
Ch 1, turn; sc in first st, (sk next 2 dc, 5 dc in next sc, sk next 2 dc, sc in next dc) {6-6}{7-7-7} times, mark center dc of last 5-dc group made for shoulder, [sk next 2 dc, (dc, 2 hdc, dc) in next sc, sk next 2 dc, sc in next dc] {2-2}{2-2-4} times, mark last sc made for collar placement, [sk next 2 dc, (dc, 2 hdc, dc) in next sc, sk next 2 dc, sc in next dc] {3-3}{3-4-4} times. Fasten off.

Row 7:
With **right** side facing, join Black with sc in marked dc for shoulder, (sk next 2 dc, 5 dc in next sc, sk next 2 dc, sc in next dc) {5-5}{6-6-6} times, sk next 2 dc, 3 dc in last sc.

Row 8:
Ch 1, turn; sc in first st, (sk next 2 dc, 5 dc in next sc, sk next 2 dc, sc in next dc) {5-5}{6-6-6} times, leave last 3 sts unworked.

Row 9:
Turn; skip first sc, sl st in next 2 dc, ch 1, sc in next dc, (sk next 2 dc, 5 dc in next sc, sk next 2 dc, sc in next dc) {4-4}{5-5-5} times, sk next 2 dc, 3 dc in last sc.

Row 10:
Ch 1, turn; sc in first st, (sk next 2 dc, 5 dc in next sc, sk next 2 dc, sc in next dc) {4-4}{5-5-5} times, leave last 3 sts unworked.

Row 11:
Ch 3, turn; 2 dc in same st, sk next 2 dc, sc in next dc, (sk next 2 dc, 5 dc in next sc, sk next 2 dc, sc in next dc) {3-3}{4-4-4} times, sk next 2 dc, 3 dc in last sc.

Row 12:
Ch 1, turn; sc in first st, * sk next 2 dc, 5 dc in next sc, sk next 2 dc, sc in next dc, rep from * across.

Rows 13 thru {17-17}{17-19-19}:
Rep Rows 11 and 12, {2-2}{2-3-3} times, then rep Row 11 once **more**.

Finishing Row:
Ch 1, turn; sc in first st, * sk next 2 dc, (dc, 2 hdc, dc) in next sc, sk next 2 dc, sc in next dc, rep from * across. Fasten off.

LEFT FRONT
With Black, ch {94-102} {110-126-142}.

Row 1 (right side):
Sc in second ch from hook, (sk next 3 chs, 5 dc in next ch, sk next 3 chs, sc in next ch) {11-12}{13-15-17} times, sk next 3 chs, 3 dc in last ch.

NOTE: Mark Row 1 as **right** side.

Row 2:
Ch 1, turn; sc in first st, (sk next 2 dc, 5 dc in next sc, sk next 2 dc, sc in next dc) {11-12}{13-15-17} times, sk next 2 dc, 3 dc in last sc.

Row 3 (Button Row):
Ch 1, turn; sc in first st, (sk next 2 dc, 5 dc in next sc, sk next 2 dc, sc in next dc) {5-6}{7-8-9} times, mark last 5-dc group made for button placement, (sk next 2 dc, 5 dc in next sc, sk next 2 dc, sc in next dc) {6-6}{6-7-8} times, mark last 5-dc group made for button placement, sk next 2 dc, 3 dc in last sc.

Rows 3a and 3b:
Medium, Large, and X-Large Only:
Ch 1, turn; sc in first st, (sk next 2 dc, 5 dc in next sc, sk next 2 dc, sc in next dc) {13-15-17} times, sk next 2 dc, 3 dc in last sc.

Row 4:
Ch 1, turn; sc in first st, (sk next 2 dc, 5 dc in next sc, sk next 2 dc, sc in next dc) {11-12}{13-15-17} times, sk next 2 dc, 4 dc in last sc.

Row 5:
Ch 3, turn; sc in next dc, (sk next 2 dc, 5 dc in next sc, sk next 2 dc, sc in next dc) {11-12}{13-15-17} times, sk next 2 dc, 3 dc in last sc.

Row 6:
Ch 1, turn; sc in first st, (sk next 2 dc, 5 dc in next sc, sk next 2 dc, sc in next dc) {11-12}{13-15-17} times, sk next 2 dc, (4 dc, hdc) in next sc, sl st in last dc.

Row 7:
Turn; sl st in first hdc, ch 4, 2 dc in same st, sk next dc, sc in next dc, (sk next 2 dc, 5 dc in next sc, sk next 2 dc, sc in next dc) {11-12}{13-15-17} times, sk next 2 dc, 3 dc in last sc.

Row 8:
Ch 1, turn; sc in first st, * sk next 2 dc, 5 dc in next sc, sk next 2 dc, sc in next dc, rep from * across.

Row 9:
Ch 3, turn; 2 dc in same st, sk next 2 dc, sc in next dc, (sk next 2 dc, 5 dc in next sc, sk next 2 dc, sc in next dc) {11-12}{13-15-17} times, sk next 2 dc, 3 dc in last sc.

Row 10:
Rep Row 8.

Row 11:
Ch 3, turn; 3 dc in same st, sk next 2 dc, sc in next dc, (sk next 2 dc, 5 dc in next sc, sk next 2 dc, sc in next dc) {11-12}{13-15-17} times, sk next 2 dc, 3 dc in last sc.

Row 12:
Ch 1, turn; sc in first st, (sk next 2 dc, 5 dc in next sc, sk next 2 dc, sc in next dc) {12-13}{14-16-18} times, dc in last dc.

Row 13 (Button Row):
Turn; sk first dc, (hdc, 4 dc) in next sc, sk next 2 dc, sc in next dc, (sk next 2 dc, 5 dc in next sc, sk next 2 dc, sc in next dc) {5-6}{7-8-9} times, mark last 5-dc group made for button placement, (sk next 2 dc, 5 dc in next sc, sk next 2 dc, sc in next dc) {6-6}{6-7-8} times, mark last 5-dc group made for button placement, sk next 2 dc, 3 dc in last sc.

Row 14:
Ch 1, turn; sc in first st, (sk next 2 dc, 5 dc in next sc, sk next 2 dc, sc in next dc) {12-13}{14-16-18} times, sk next dc, (2 dc, tr) in last hdc.

Rows 15-17:
Ch 1, turn; sc in first st, (sk next 2 dc, 5 dc in next sc, sk next 2 dc, sc in next dc) {12-13}{14-16-18} times, sk next 2 dc, 3 dc in last sc.

Row 18:
Ch 1, turn; sc in first st, (sk next 2 dc, 5 dc in next sc, sk next 2 dc, sc in next dc) {12-13}{14-16-18} times, sk next 2 dc, 4 dc in last sc.

Row 19:
Ch 3, turn; sc in next dc, (sk next 2 dc, 5 dc in next sc, sk next 2 dc, sc in next dc) {12-13}{14-16-18} times, sk next 2 dc, 3 dc in last sc.

Row 20:
Ch 1, turn; sc in first st, (sk next 2 dc, 5 dc in next sc, sk next 2 dc, sc in next dc) {12-13}{14-16-18} times, sk next 2 dc, (4 dc, hdc) in next sc, sl st in last dc.

Row 21:
Turn; sl st in first hdc, ch 4, 2 dc in same st, sk next dc, sc in next dc, (sk next 2 dc, 5 dc in next sc, sk next 2 dc, sc in next dc) {12-13}{14-16-18} times, sk next 2 dc, 3 dc in last sc.

Row 22:
Ch 1, turn; sc in first st, * sk next 2 dc, 5 dc in next sc, sk next 2 dc, sc in next st, rep from * across.

Row 23:
Ch 3, turn; 2 dc in same st, sk next 2 dc, sc in next dc, (sk next 2 dc, 5 dc in next sc, sk next 2 dc, sc in next dc) {12-13}{14-16-18} times, sk next 2 dc, 3 dc in last sc.

Rows 24 and 25:
Rep Rows 22 and 23.

X-Small Only:
Row 26:
Rep Row 22. Fasten off.

Small, Medium, Large, and X-Large Only:
Row 26:
Ch 1, turn; sc in first st, (sk next 2 dc, 5 dc in next sc, sk next 2 dc, sc in next dc) {13}{14-16-18} times, sk next 2 dc, (dc, 2 hdc, dc) in next sc, sk next 2 dc, sc in last dc. Fasten off.

Row 27:
With **right** side facing, join Black with sc in center dc of first 5-dc group, (sk next 2 dc, 5 dc in next sc, sk next 2 dc, sc in next dc) {12-12}{13-15-17} times, sk next 2 dc, 3 dc in last sc.

Row 28:
Ch 1, turn; sc in first st, (sk next 2 dc, 5 dc in next sc, sk next 2 dc, sc in next dc) {12-12}{13-15-17} times, leave last 3 sts unworked.

X-Small, Small, and Medium Only:
Row 29:
Ch 3, turn; 2 dc in same st, sk next 2 dc, sc in next dc, (sk next 2 dc, 5 dc in next sc, sk next 2 dc, sc in next dc) {11-11}{12} times, sk next 2 dc, 3 dc in last sc.

Row 30:
Ch 1, turn; sc in first st, *sk next 2 dc, 5 dc in next sc, sk next 2 dc, sc in next dc, rep from * across.

Rows 31-42:
Rep Rows 29 and 30, 6 times, do **not** fasten off.

Skip to Left Lapel Shaping.

Large and X-Large Only:
Row 29:
Ch 3, turn; dc in same st, sk next 2 dc, sc in next dc, (sk next 2 dc, 5 dc in next sc, sk next 2 dc, sc in next dc) {14-16} times, sk next 2 dc, 3 dc in last sc.

Row 30:
Ch 1, turn; sc in first st, (sk next 2 dc, 5 dc in next sc, sk next 2 dc, sc in next dc) {14-16} times, sk next 2 dc, (3 dc, hdc) in next sc, sk next dc, sl st in last dc.

Row 31:
Turn; sl st in first hdc, ch 1, sc in next st, (sk next 2 dc, 5 dc in next sc, sk next 2 dc, sc in next dc) {14-16} times, sk next 2 dc, 3 dc in last sc.

Row 32:
Ch 1, turn; sc in first st, (sk next 2 dc, 5 dc in next sc, sk next 2 dc, sc in next dc) {14-16} times, sk next 2 dc, 2 dc in last sc.

Row 33:
Turn; sk first 2 dc, (hdc, 3 dc) in next sc, sk next 2 dc, sc in next dc, (sk next 2 dc, 5 dc in next sc, sk next 2 dc, sc in next dc) {13-15} times, sk next 2 dc, 3 dc in last sc.

Row 34:
Ch 1, turn; sc in first st, (sk next 2 dc, 5 dc in next sc, sk next 2 dc, sc in next dc) {14-16} times.

Row 35:
Ch 3, turn; 2 dc in same st, sk next 2 dc, sc in next dc, (sk next 2 dc, 5 dc in next sc, sk next 2 dc, sc in next dc) {13-15} times, sk next 2 dc, 3 dc in last sc.

Rows 36 thru {42-44}:
Rep Rows 34 and 35, {3-4} times, then rep Row 34 once **more**.

LEFT LAPEL SHAPING
Row 1:
Ch 3, turn; 2 dc in same st, sk next 2 dc, sc in next dc, (sk next 2 dc, 5 dc in next sc, sk next 2 dc, sc in next dc) {11-11}{12-13-15} times, sk next 2 dc, dc in last sc.

15

Row 2:
Ch 3, turn; dc in same st, dc in next sc, sk next 2 dc, sc in next dc, * sk next 2 dc, 5 dc in next sc, sk next 2 dc, sc in next dc, rep from * across.

Row 3:
Ch 3, turn; 2 dc in same st, sk next 2 dc, sc in next dc, * sk next 2 dc, 5 dc in next sc, sk next 2 dc, sc in next dc, rep from * across.

Row 4:
Ch 3, turn; sk next 2 dc, sc in next dc, * sk next 2 dc, 5 dc in next sc, sk next 2 dc, sc in next dc, rep from * across.

Row 5:
Ch 3, turn; 2 dc in same st, sk next 2 dc, sc in next dc, (sk next 2 dc, 5 dc in next sc, sk next 2 dc, sc in next dc) {10-10}{11-12-14} times, sk next 2 dc, dc in next sc, 2 dc in last dc.

Row 6:
Ch 1, turn; sc in first st, [sk next 2 dc, (dc, 2 hdc, dc) in next sc, sk next 2 dc, sc in next dc] {3-3}{3-4-4} times, mark last sc made for collar placement, [sk next 2 dc, (dc, 2 hdc, dc) in next sc, sk next 2 dc, sc in next dc] {2-2}{2-2-4} times, * sk next 2 dc, 5 dc in next sc, sk next 2 dc, sc in next dc, rep from * across.

Row 7:
Ch 3, turn; 2 dc in same st, sk next 2 dc, sc in next dc, (sk next 2 dc, 5 dc in next sc, sk next 2 dc, sc in next dc) {5-5}{6-6-6} times.

Row 8:
Turn; skip first sc, sl st in next 2 dc, ch 1, sc in next dc, * sk next 2 dc, 5 dc in next sc, sk next 2 dc, sc in next dc, rep from * across.

Row 9:
Ch 3, turn; 2 dc in same st, sk next 2 dc, sc in next dc, (sk next 2 dc, 5 dc in next sc, sk next 2 dc, sc in next dc) {4-4}{5-5-5} times.

Row 10:
Turn; sk first sc, sl st in next 2 dc, ch 1, sc in next dc, * sk next 2 dc, 5 dc in next sc, sk next 2 dc, sc in next dc, rep from * across.

Row 11:
Ch 3, turn; 2 dc in same st, sk next 2 dc, sc in next dc, (sk next 2 dc, 5 dc in next sc, sk next 2 dc, sc in next dc) {3-3}{4-4-4} times, sk next 2 dc, 3 dc in last sc.

Row 12:
Ch 1, turn; sc in first st, * sk next 2 dc, 5 dc in next sc, sk next 2 dc, sc in next dc, rep from * across.

Row 13 thru {17-17}{17-19-19}:
Rep Rows 11 and 12, {2-2}{2-3-3} times, then rep Row 11 once **more**.

Finishing Row:
Ch 1, turn; sc in first st, * sk next 2 dc, (dc, 2 hdc, dc) in next sc, sk next 2 dc, sc in next dc, rep from * across. Fasten off.

Sew Right Front and Left Front to Back at sides and shoulders.

BOTTOM BORDER

Row 1:
With **right** side facing and working in free loops of beginning ch *(Fig. 3b, page 95)*, join Red with slip st in ch at base of 3 dc on bottom corner of Left Front, ch 4, dc in same ch, ch 1, † sk next 3 chs, sc in next ch, ch 1, sk next 3 chs, (dc, ch 1) 3 times in next ch †, rep from † to † {10-11} {12-14-16} times **more**, sk next 3 chs, sc in side seam, ch 1, sk next 3 chs, (dc, ch 1) 3 times in next ch, rep from † to † {14-16}{18-20-22} times, sk next 3 chs, sc in side seam, ch 1, sk next 3 chs, (dc, ch 1) 3 times in next ch, rep from † to † {10-11}{12-14-16} times, sk next 3 chs, sc in next ch, sk next 3 chs, (dc, ch 1, dc) in last ch changing to Yellow in last dc *(Fig. 4, page 95)*: {152-168}{184-208-232} ch-1 sps.

Row 2:
Ch 1, turn; sc in first st, * ch 3, (YO, sk next ch-1 sp, pull up a loop in next st, YO, pull through 2 loops on hook) 3 times, YO, pull through all 4 loops on hook, ch 3, sk next ch-1 sp, sc in next st, rep from * across, changing to Black in last sc.

Row 3:
Ch 4, turn; dc in same st, ch 1, * sk next ch-3 sp, sc in next st, ch 1, sk next ch-3 sp, (dc, ch 1) 3 times in next sc, rep from * {36-40}{44-50-56} times **more**, ch 1, sk next ch-3 sp, sc in next st, ch 1, sk next ch-3 sp, (dc, ch 1, dc) in last sc.

Row 4:
Rep Row 2, changing to Red in last sc.

Row 5:
Rep Row 3, changing to Yellow in last sc.

Row 6:
Rep Row 2.

Row 7:
Rep Row 3.

Row 8:
Rep Row 2, do **not** change colors at end of row.

Row 9:
Ch 1, turn; sc in first st, † [(ch 3, sc in next sp) twice, ch 3, sc in next sc] 6 times †, * ch 3, sc in next ch-3 sp, ch 3, sc in next st, ch 3, sc in next ch-3 sp, ch 3, sc in next sc, rep from * {25-29}{33-39-45} times **more**, then rep from † to † once: {140-156} {172-196-220} ch-3 sps.

Row 10:
Ch 4, turn; sc in next sp, * ch 3, sc in next sp, rep from * across, ch 1, dc in last sc.

Row 11:
Ch 1, turn; sc in first st, sk next ch-1 sp and next sc, (2 hdc, ch 2, 2 dc) in next ch-3 sp, dc in next ch-3 sp, * (2 dc, ch 2, 2 dc) in next ch-3 sp, dc in next ch-3 sp, rep from * {67-75}{83-95-107} times more, (2 dc, ch 2, 2 hdc) in next ch-3 sp, sk next sc, sc in third ch of turning ch-4.

Row 12:
Turn; sk first sc, sl st in next 2 hdc, sl st in next ch-2 sp and in next 2 dc, ch 1, sc in next dc, sk next 2 dc, (2 hdc, ch 2, 2 dc) in next ch-2 sp, sk next 2 dc, dc in next dc, * sk next 2 dc, (2 dc, ch 2, 2 dc) in next ch-2 sp, sk next 2 dc, dc in next dc, rep from * {65-73}{81-93-105} times **more**, sk next 2 dc, (2 dc, ch 2, 2 hdc) in next ch-2 sp, sk next 2 dc, sc in next dc, leave last 5 sts unworked.

Row 13:
Turn; sk first sc, sl st in next 2 hdc, sl st in next ch-2 sp and in next 2 dc, ch 1, sc in next dc, sk next 2 dc, (2 hdc, ch 2, 2 dc) in next ch-2 sp, sk next 2 dc, dc in next dc, * sk next 2 dc, (2 dc, ch 2, 2 dc) in next ch-2 sp, sk next 2 dc, dc in next dc, rep from * {63-71}{79-91-103} times **more**, sk next 2 dc, (2 dc, ch 2, 2 hdc) in next ch-2 sp, sk next 2 dc, sc in next dc, leave last 5 sts unworked.

Row 14:

Turn; sk first sc, sl st in next 2 hdc, sl st in next ch-2 sp and in next 2 dc, ch 1, sc in next dc, sk next 2 dc, (2 hdc, ch 2, 2 dc) in next ch-2 sp, sk next 2 dc, dc in next dc, * sk next 2 dc, (2 dc, ch 2, 2 dc) in next ch-2 sp, sk next 2 dc, dc in next dc, rep from * {61-69}{77-89-101} times **more**, sk next 2 dc, (2 dc, ch 2, 2 hdc) in next ch-2 sp, sk next 2 dc, sc in next dc, leave last 5 sts unworked.

Row 15:

Turn; sk first sc, sl st in next 2 hdc, sl st in next ch-2 sp and in next 2 dc, ch 1, sc in next dc, sk next 2 dc, (2 hdc, ch 2, 2 dc) in next ch-2 sp, sk next 2 dc, dc in next dc, * sk next 2 dc, (2 dc, ch 2, 2 dc) in next ch-2 sp, sk next 2 dc, dc in next dc, rep from * {59-67}{75-87-99} times **more**, sk next 2 dc, (2 dc, ch 2, 2 hdc) in next ch-2 sp, sk next 2 dc, sc in next dc, leave last 5 sts unworked.

Row 16:

Turn; skip first sc, sl st in next 2 hdc, sl st in next ch-2 sp and in next 2 dc, ch 1, sc in next dc, sk next 2 dc, (2 hdc, ch 2, 2 dc) in next ch-2 sp, sk next 2 dc, dc in next dc, * sk next 2 dc, (2 dc, ch 2, 2 dc) in next ch-2 sp, sk next 2 dc, dc in next dc, rep from * {57-65}{73-85-97} times **more**, sk next 2 dc, (2 dc, ch 2, 2 hdc) in next ch-2 sp, sk next 2 dc, sc in next dc, leave last 5 sts unworked.

Row 17:

Turn; skip first sc, sl st in next 2 hdc, sl st in next ch-2 sp and in next 2 dc, ch 1, sc in next dc, sk next 2 dc, (2 hdc, ch 2, 2 dc) in next ch-2 sp, sk next 2 dc, dc in next dc, * sk next 2 dc, (2 dc, ch 2, 2 dc) in next ch-2 sp, sk next 2 dc, dc in next dc, rep from * {55-63}{71-83-95} times **more**, sk next 2 dc, (2 dc, ch 2, 2 hdc) in next ch-2 sp, sk 2 dc, sc in next dc, leave last 5 sts unworked.

Row 18:

Turn; sk first sc, sl st in next 2 hdc, sl st in next ch-2 sp and in next 2 dc, ch 1, sc in next dc, sk next 2 dc, (2 hdc, ch 2, 2 dc) in next ch-2 sp, sk next 2 dc, dc in next dc, * sk next 2 dc, (2 dc, ch 2, 2 dc) in next ch-2 sp, sk next 2 dc, dc in next dc, rep from * {53-61}{69-81-93} times **more**, sk next 2 dc, (2 dc, ch 2, 2 hdc) in next ch-2 sp, sk next 2 dc, sc in next dc, leave last 5 sts unworked.

Row 19:

Turn; skip first sc, sl st in next 2 hdc, sl st in next ch-2 sp and in next 2 dc, ch 1, sc in next dc, sk next 2 dc, (2 hdc, ch 2, 2 dc) in next ch-2 sp, sk next 2 dc, dc in next dc, * sk next 2 dc, (2 dc, ch 2, hdc in top of dc just made, 2 dc) in next ch-2 sp, sk next 2 dc, dc in next dc, rep from * {51-59}{67-79-91} times **more**, sk next 2 dc, (2 dc, ch 2, 2 hdc) in next ch-2 sp, sk next 2 dc, sc in next dc, leave last 5 sts unworked. Fasten off.

SLEEVE (make 2)

With Black, ch {92-108}{108-124-140}.

Row 1 (right side):

2 dc in fourth ch from hook, (sk next 3 chs, sc in next ch, sk next 3 chs, 5 dc in next ch) {10-12}{12-14-16} times, sk next 3 chs, sc in next ch, sk next 3 chs, 3 dc in last ch.

NOTE: Mark Row 1 as **right** side.

Row 2:

Ch 1, turn; sc in first st, * sk next 2 dc, 5 dc in next sc, sk next 2 dc, sc in next st, rep from * across.

Row 3:

Ch 3, turn; 2 dc in same st, sk next 2 dc, sc in next dc, (sk next 2 dc, 5 dc in next sc, sk next 2 dc, sc in next dc) {10-12}{12-14-16} times, sk next 2 dc, 3 dc in last sc.

18

Row 4-6:
Rep Rows 2 and 3 once, then rep Row 2 once **more**.

Row 6a:
Large and X-Large Only:
Ch 3, turn; 2 dc in same st, sk next 2 dc, sc in next dc, (sk next 2 dc, 5 dc in next sc, sk next 2 dc, sc in next dc) {14-16} times, sk next 2 dc, 3 dc in last sc.

Row 6b:
Large and X-Large Only:
Rep Row 2.

Row 7:
Ch 3, turn; 3 dc in same st, sk next 2 dc, sc in next dc, (sk next 2 dc, 5 dc in next sc, sk next 2 dc, sc in next dc) {10-12}{12-14-16} times, sk next 2 dc, 4 dc in last sc.

Row 8:
Ch 3, turn; sc in next st, (sk next 2 dc, 5 dc in next sc, sk next 2 dc, sc in next dc) {11-13}{13-15-17} times, dc in last dc.

Row 9:
Turn; sk first dc, (hdc, 4 dc) in next sc, sk next 2 dc, sc in next dc, (sk next 2 dc, 5 dc in next sc, sk next 2 dc, sc in next dc) {10-12}{12-14-16} times, sk next 2 dc, (4 dc, hdc) in next sc, sl st in last dc.

Row 10:
Turn; sl st in first hdc, ch 4, 2 dc in same st, sk next dc, sc in next dc, (sk next 2 dc, 5 dc in next sc, sk next 2 dc, sc in next dc) {11-13}{13-15-17} times, sk next dc, (2 dc, tr) in last hdc.

Row 11:
Rep Row 2.

Row 12:
Ch 3, turn; 2 dc in same st, sk next 2 dc, sc in next dc, (sk next 2 dc, 5 dc in next sc, sk next 2 dc, sc in next dc) {11-13}{13-15-17} times, sk next 2 dc, 3 dc in last sc.

Row 13:
Rep Row 2.

Row 14:
Ch 3, turn; 3 dc in same st, sk next 2 dc, sc in next dc, (sk next 2 dc, 5 dc in next sc, sk next 2 dc, sc in next dc) {11-13}{13-15-17} times, sk next 2 dc, 4 dc in last sc.

Row 15:
Ch 3, turn; sc in next st, (sk next 2 dc, 5 dc in next sc, sk next 2 dc, sc in next dc) {12-14}{14-16-18} times, dc in last dc.

Row 16:
Turn; sk first dc, (hdc, 4 dc) in next sc, sk next 2 dc, sc in next dc, (sk next 2 dc, 5 dc in next sc, sk next 2 dc, sc in next dc) {11-13}{13-15-17} times, sk next 2 dc, (4 dc, hdc) in next sc, sl st in last dc.

Row 17:
Turn; sl st in first hdc, ch 4, 2 dc in same st, sk next dc, sc in next dc, (sk next 2 dc, 5 dc in next sc, sk next 2 dc, sc in next dc) {12-14}{14-16-18} times, sk next dc, (2 dc, tr) in last hdc.

Row 18:
Rep Row 2.

Row 19:
Ch 3, turn; 2 dc in same st, sk next 2 dc, sc in next dc, (sk next 2 dc, 5 dc in next sc, sk next 2 dc, sc in next dc) {12-14}{14-16-18} times, sk next 2 dc, 3 dc in last sc.

Row 20:
Rep Row 2.

Row 21:
Ch 3, turn; 3 dc in same st, sk next 2 dc, sc in next dc, (sk next 2 dc, 5 dc in next sc, sk next 2 dc, sc in next dc) {12-14}{14-16-18} times, sk next 2 dc, 4 dc in last sc.

Row 22:
Ch 3, turn; sc in next st, (sk next 2 dc, 5 dc in next sc, sk next 2 dc, sc in next dc) {13-15}{15-17-19} times, dc in last dc.

Row 23:
Turn; sk first dc, (hdc, 4 dc) in next sc, sk next 2 dc, sc in next dc, (sk next 2 dc, 5 dc in next sc, sk next 2 dc, sc in next dc) {12-14}{14-16-18} times, sk next 2 dc, (4 dc, hdc) in next sc, sl st in last dc.

Row 24:
Turn; sl st in first hdc, ch 4, 2 dc in same st, sk next dc, sc in next dc, (sk next 2 dc, 5 dc in next sc, sk next 2 dc, sc in next dc) {13-15}{15-17-19} times, sk next dc, (2 dc, tr) in last hdc.

Row 25:
Ch 1, turn; sc in first st, * sk next 2 dc, 5 dc in next sc, sk next 2 dc, sc in next st, rep from * across.

Row 26:
Ch 3, turn; 2 dc in same st, sk next 2 dc, sc in next dc, (sk next 2 dc, 5 dc in next sc, sk next 2 dc, sc in next dc) {13-15}{15-17-19} times, sk next 2 dc, 3 dc in last sc.

Rows 27-30:
Rep Rows 25 and 26 twice.

X-Small Only:
Row 31:
Ch 1, turn; sc in first st, (sk next 2 dc, 5 dc in next sc, sk next 2 dc, sc in next dc) 14 times, mark center dc of last 5-dc group made. Fasten off.

Small, Medium, Large, and X-Large Only:
Row 31:
Ch 1, turn; sc in first st, sk next 2 dc, (dc, 2 hdc, dc) in next sc, sk next 2 dc, sc in next dc, (sk next 2 dc, 5 dc in next sc, sk next 2 dc, sc in next dc) {14}{14-16-18} times, mark center dc of last 5-dc group made, sk next 2 dc, (dc, 2 hdc, dc) in next sc, sk next 2 dc, sc in last dc. Fasten off.

Row 32:
With **wrong** side facing, join Black with sc in marked dc, (sk next 2 dc, 5 dc in next sc, sk next 2 dc, sc in next dc) {13-13}{13-15-17} times, leave last {3-5}{5-5-5} sts unworked.

Row 33:
Turn; sk first sc, sl st in next 2 dc, ch 1, sc in next dc, (sk next 2 dc, 5 dc in next sc, sk next 2 dc, sc in next dc) {12-12}{12-14-16} times, leave last 3 sts unworked.

Row 34:
Ch 3, turn; dc in same st, sk next 2 dc, sc in next dc, (sk next 2 dc, 5 dc in next sc, sk next 2 dc, sc in next dc) {11-11}{11-13-15} times, sk next 2 dc, 2 dc in next sc, leave last 3 sts unworked.

Row 35:
Turn; sk first 2 dc, (hdc, 3 dc) in next sc, sk next 2 dc, sc in next dc, (sk next 2 dc, 5 dc in next sc, sk next 2 dc, sc in next dc) {10-10}{10-12-14} times, sk next 2 dc, (3 dc, hdc) in next sc, sk next dc, sl st in last dc.

Row 36:
Turn; sl st in first hdc, ch 1, sc in next dc, (sk next 2 dc, 5 dc in next sc, sk next 2 dc, sc in next dc) {11-11}{11-13-15} times, leave last hdc unworked.

Row 37:
Ch 3, turn; dc in same st, sk next 2 dc, sc in next dc, (sk next 2 dc, 5 dc in next sc, sk next 2 dc, sc in next dc) {10-10}{10-12-14} times, sk next 2 dc, 2 dc in last sc.

Row 38:
Turn; sk first 2 dc, (hdc, 3 dc) in next sc, sk next 2 dc, sc in next dc, (sk next 2 dc, 5 dc in next sc, sk next 2 dc, sc in next dc) {9-9}{9-11-13} times, sk next 2 dc, (3 dc, hdc) in next sc, sl st in last dc.

Row 39:
Turn; sl st in first hdc, ch 1, sc in next dc, (sk next 2 dc, 5 dc in next sc, sk next 2 dc, sc in next dc) {10-10}{10-12-14} times, leave last hdc unworked.

Row 40:
Ch 3, turn; dc in same st, sk next 2 dc, sc in next dc, (sk next 2 dc, 5 dc in next sc, sk next 2 dc, sc in next dc) {9-9}{9-11-13} times, sk next 2 dc, 2 dc in last sc.

Row 41:
Turn; sk first 2 dc, (hdc, 3 dc) in next sc, sk next 2 dc, sc in next dc, (sk next 2 dc, 5 dc in next sc, sk next 2 dc, sc in next dc) {8-8}{8-10-12} times, sk next 2 dc, (3 dc, hdc) in next sc, sl st in last dc.

Row 42:
Turn; sl st in first hdc, ch 1, sc in next dc, (sk next 2 dc, 5 dc in next sc, sk next 2 dc, sc in next dc) {9-9} {9-11-13} times, leave last hdc unworked.

Row 43:
X-Small, Small, and Medium Only:
Turn; sk first sc, sl st in next 2 dc, ch 1, sc in next dc, (sk next 2 dc, 5 dc in next sc, sk next 2 dc, sc in next dc) 8 times, leave last 3 sts unworked.

Large and X-Large Only:
Ch 3, turn; dc in same st, sk next 2 dc, sc in next dc, (sk next 2 dc, 5 dc in next sc, sk next 2 dc, sc in next dc) {10-12} times, sk next 2 dc, 2 dc in last sc.

Row 44:
X-Small, Small, and Medium Only:
Turn; sk first sc, sl st in next 2 dc, ch 1, sc in next dc, (sk next 2 dc, 5 dc in next sc, sk next 2 dc, sc in next dc) 7 times, leave last 3 sts unworked.

Large and X-Large Only:
Turn; sk first 2 dc, (hdc, 3 dc) in next sc, sk next 2 dc, sc in next dc, (sk next 2 dc, 5 dc in next sc, sk next 2 dc, sc in next dc) {9-11} times, sk next 2 dc, (3 dc, hdc) in next sc, sl st in last dc.

Row 45:
X-Small, Small, and Medium Only:
Turn; sk first sc, sl st in next 2 dc, ch 1, sc in next dc, (sk next 2 dc, 5 dc in next sc, sk next 2 dc, sc in next dc) 6 times, leave last 3 sts unworked.

Large and X-Large Only:
Turn; sl st in first hdc, ch 1, sc in next st, (sk next 2 dc, 5 dc in next sc, sk next 2 dc, sc in next dc) {10-12} times, leave last hdc unworked.

Row 46:
Turn; sk first sc, sl st in next 2 dc, ch 1, sc in next dc, (sk next 2 dc, 5 dc in next sc, sk next 2 dc, sc in next dc) {5-5}{5-9-11} times, leave last 3 sts unworked.

Row 47:
X-Small, Small, and Medium Only:
Turn; sk first sc, sl st in next 3 dc, sk next 2 dc, (hdc, 3 dc) in next sc, sk next 2 dc, sc in next dc, (sk next 2 dc, 5 dc in next sc, sk next 2 dc, sc in next dc) twice, sk next 2 dc, (3 dc, hdc) in next sc, sk next 2 dc, sl st in next dc, leave last 3 sts unworked.

Large and X-Large Only:
Turn; sk first sc, sl st in next 2 dc, ch 1, sc in next dc, (sk next 2 dc, 5 dc in next sc, sk next 2 dc, sc in next dc) {8-10} times, leave last 3 sts unworked.

Row 48:
X-Small, Small, and Medium Only:
Turn; sk first sl st, sl st in next hdc and in next 2 dc, sk next dc, (hdc, 2 dc) in next sc, sk next 2 dc, sc in next dc, sk next 2 dc, (dc, 2 hdc, dc) in next sc, sk next 2 dc, sc in next dc, sk next 2 dc, (2 dc, hdc) in next sc, sk next dc, sl st in next dc, leave last 2 sts unworked. Fasten off.
Large and X-Large Only:
Turn; sk first sc, sl st in next 2 dc, ch 1, sc in next dc, (sk next 2 dc, 5 dc in next sc, sk next 2 dc, sc in next dc) {7-9} times, leave last 3 sts unworked.

Row 49:
Large and X-Large Only:
Turn; sk first sc, sl st in next 2 dc, ch 1, sc in next dc, (sk next 2 dc, 5 dc in next sc, sk next 2 dc, sc in next dc) {6-8} times, leave last 3 sts unworked.

Row 50:
Large and X-Large Only:
Turn; sk first sc, sl st in next 3 dc, sk next 2 dc, (hdc, 3 dc) in next sc, sk next 2 dc, sc in next dc, (sk next 2 dc, 5 dc in next sc, sk next 2 dc, sc in next dc) {3-5} times, sk next 2 dc, (3 dc, hdc) in next sc, sk next 2 dc, sl st in next dc, leave last 3 sts unworked.

Row 51:
Large Only:
Turn; sl st in first hdc and in next 2 dc, sk next dc, (hdc, 2 dc) in next sc, sk next 2 dc, sc in next dc, [sk next 2 dc, (dc, 2 hdc, dc) in next sc, sk next 2 dc, sc in next dc] twice, sk next 2 dc, (2 dc, hdc) in next sc, sk next dc, sl st in next dc, leave last 2 sts unworked. Fasten off.

X-Large Only:
Turn; sl st in first hdc and in next 2 dc, sk next dc, (hdc, 2 dc) in next sc, sk next 2 dc, sc in next dc, sk next 2 dc, (hdc, 3 dc) in next sc, sk next 2 dc, sc in next dc, (sk next 2 dc, 5 dc in next sc, sk next 2 dc, sc in next dc) twice, sk next 2 dc, (3 dc, hdc) in next sc, sk next 2 dc, sc in next dc, sk next 2 dc, (2 dc, hdc) in next sc, sk next dc, sl st in next dc, leave last 2 sts unworked.

Row 52:
X-Large Only:
Turn; sl st in first 7 sts, sk next dc, (hdc, 2 dc) in next sc, sk next 2 dc, sc in next dc, [sk next 2 dc, (dc, 2 hdc, dc) in next sc, sk next 2 dc, sc in next dc] twice, sk next 2 dc, (2 dc, hdc) in next sc, sk next dc, sl st in next dc. Fasten off.

Sew sleeves together along side seams.

SLEEVE BORDER
Rnd 1:
With **right** side facing and working in free loops of beginning ch, join Red with sl st at seam, ch 4, dc in same sp, [sk next 3 chs, sc in next ch, sk next 3 chs, (dc, ch 1, dc, ch 1, dc) in next ch] {10-12}{12-14-16} times, sk next 3 chs, sc in next ch, dc in same sp as beg ch 4, ch 1, join with sl st in third ch of beg ch 4, changing to Yellow.

Rnd 2:
Ch 1, sc in same st, *† ch 2, (YO, pull up a loop in next st, YO, pull through 2 loops on hook) 3 times, YO, pull through all loops on hook, ch 2 †, sc in next dc, rep from * {9-11}{11-13-15} times **more**, then rep from † to † once, join with sl st in beg sc, changing to Black.

Rnd 3:
Ch 4, dc in same st, [sk next ch-2 sp, sc in next st, sk next ch-2 sp, (dc, ch 1, dc, ch 1, dc) in next sc] {10-12}{12-14-16} times, sk next ch-2 sp, sc in next st, dc in same sp as beg ch 4, ch 1, join with sl st in third ch of beg ch-4.

Rnd 4:
Rep Rnd 2, changing to Red.

Rnd 5:
Ch 4, dc in same st, [sk next ch-2 sp, sc in next st, sk next ch-2 sp, (dc, ch 1, dc, ch 1, dc) in next sc] {10-12}{12-14-16} times, sk next ch-2 sp, sc in next st, dc in same st as beg ch 4, ch 1, join with sl st in third ch of beg ch-4, changing to Yellow.

Rnds 6-8:
Rep Rnds 2-4, do **not** change colors at end of last rnd.

Rnd 9:
Ch 1, sc in same st, ch 3, sc in next sp, ch 3, sc in next sc, ch 3, sc in next sp, * ch 3, sc in next st, ch 3, sc in next sp, ch 3, sc in next sc, ch 3, sc in next sp, rep from * around, join with dc in beg sc.

Rnd 10:
Ch 1, sc in last sp made, ch 3, * sc in next sp, ch 3, rep from * around, join with sl st in beg sc.

Rnd 11:
Sl st in next sp, ch 3, (2 dc, ch 2, 2 dc) in next sp, * dc in next sp, (2 dc, ch 2, 2 dc) in next sp, rep from * around, join with sl st in first dc.

Rnds 12-21:
Ch 3, sk next 2 dc, (2 dc, ch 2, 2 dc) in next ch-2 sp, * sk next 2 dc, dc in next dc, sk next 2 dc, (2 dc, ch 2, 2 dc) in next ch-2 sp, rep from * around, join with sl st in first dc.

Rnd 22:
Ch 3, sk next 2 dc, (2 dc, ch 2, hdc in top of last dc made, 2 dc) in next ch-2 sp, * sk next 2 dc, dc in next dc, sk next 2 dc, (2 dc, ch 2, hdc in top of last dc made, 2 dc) in next ch-2 sp, rep from * around, join with sl st in first dc. Fasten off.

Sew sleeves into sleeve openings.

COLLAR
With Black, ch {146-146} {146-158-194}.

Row 1 (right side):
Sc in second ch from hook and each ch across: {145-145}{145-157-193} sc.

NOTE: Mark Row 1 as **right** side.

Row 2:
Ch 3, turn; 3 dc in same st, sk next 2 sc, sc in next sc, (sk next 2 sc, 5 dc in next sc, sk next 2 sc, sc in next sc) {23-23}{23-25-31} times, sk next 2 sc, 4 dc in last sc.

Row 3:
Ch 3, turn; sc in next dc, (sk next 2 dc, 5 dc in next sc, sk next 2 dc, sc in next dc) {24-24}{24-26-32} times, dc in last dc.

Row 4:
Turn; sk first dc, (hdc, 4 dc) in next sc, sk next 2 dc, sc in next dc, (sk next 2 dc, 5 dc in next sc, sk next 2 dc, sc in next dc) {23-23}{23-25-31} times, sk next 2 dc, (4 dc, hdc) in next sc, sl st in last dc.

Row 5:
Turn; (sl st, ch 4, 2 dc) in first hdc, sk next dc, sc in next dc, (sk next 2 dc, 5 dc in next sc, sk next 2 dc, sc in next dc) {24-24}{24-26-32} times, (2 dc, tr) in last hdc.

Row 6:
Ch 1, turn; sc in first st, * sk next 2 dc, 5 dc in next sc, sk next 2 dc, sc in next st, rep from * across.

Row 7:
Ch 3, turn; 3 dc in same st, sk next 2 dc, sc in next dc, (sk next 2 dc, 5 dc in next sc, sk next 2 dc, sc in next dc) {24-24}{24-26-32} times, sk next 2 dc, 4 dc in last dc.

Row 8:
Ch 3, turn; sc in next st, (sk next 2 dc, 5 dc in next sc, sk next 2 dc, sc in next dc) {25-25}{25-27-33} times, dc in last dc.

Row 9:
Turn; sk first dc, (hdc, 4 dc) in next sc, sk next 2 dc, sc in next dc, (sk next 2 dc, 5 dc in next sc, sk next 2 dc, sc in next dc) {24-24}{24-26-32} times, sk next 2 dc, (4 dc, hdc) in next sc, sl st in last dc.

Row 10:
Turn; (sl st, ch 4, 2 dc) in next hdc, sk next dc, sc in next dc, (sk next 2 dc, 5 dc in next sc, sk next 2 dc, sc in next dc) {25-25}{25-27-33} times, (2 dc, tr) in last hdc.

Row 11:
Ch 1, turn; sc in first st, * sk next 2 dc, (dc, 2 hdc, dc) in next sc, sk next 2 dc, sc in next st, rep from * across. Fasten off.

With **right** side of Collar facing **wrong** side of Jacket and matching ends of Collar with marked sts, sew Collar to Jacket. Turn Collar to outside.

Sew buttons to marked sts.

skirt

FINISHED HIP SIZE:

X-Small:	39" (99 cm)	Large:	48" (122 cm)
Small:	42" (106.5 cm)	X-Large:	51" (129.5 cm)
Medium:	45" (114.5 cm)		

Instructions are written with sizes X-Small and Small in the first set of braces { } and with sizes Medium, Large, and X-Large in the second set of braces. Instructions will be easier to read if you circle all the numbers pertaining to your size. If only one number is given, it applies to all sizes.

MATERIALS

Bedspread Weight Cotton Thread (size 10)
[350 yards (320 meters) per ball]:
Black - {5-6}{6-7-7} balls
Red - 2 balls
Yellow - {1-1}{2-2-2} balls
Steel crochet hook, size 7 (1.65 mm)
or size needed for gauge
Sewing needle and matching thread
Lightweight material for lining
Skirt pattern for lining (Butterick #3134 used for model)

GAUGE:

Motif measures 3" (7.5 cm) square.

SPECIAL STITCHES:

2dctog: (YO, insert hook in specified sp, YO, pull up a loop, YO, pull through 2 loops on hook) twice, YO, pull through all loops on hook.

3dctog: (YO, insert hook in specified sp, YO, pull up a loop, YO, pull through 2 loops on hook) 3 times, YO, pull through all loops on hook.

Sl st in center of sc just made: Insert hook through one horizontal bar and one vertical bar of specified st *(Fig. 5, page 95)*, YO, pull through all loops on hook.

Hdc in top of dc just made: YO, insert hook through one horizontal bar and one vertical bar of specified stitch *(Fig 5, page 95)*, YO, pull up a loop, YO, pull through all loops on hook.

Dc in top of dc just made: YO, insert hook through one horizontal bar and one vertical bar of specified stitch *(Fig 5, page 95)*, YO, pull up a loop, YO, pull through 2 loops on hook, YO, pull through rem loops on hook.

DRAWSTRING

With Black, ch 3, dc in third ch from hook, * ch 2, dc in top of dc just made, rep from * until drawstring measures {45-48}{51-54-57}"/ {114.5-122}{129.5-137-145} cm. Fasten off. Trim ends.

WAISTBAND

With Black, ch {234-252} {270-288-306}, join with sl st to form ring taking care not to twist ch.

Rnd 1:

Ch 4 (**counts as first dc plus ch 1, now and throughout**), sk next ch, * dc in next ch, ch 1, sk next ch, rep from * around, join with sl st in first dc: {117-126}{135-144-153} dc.

Rnds 2-5:

Sl st in first sp, ch 4, * dc in next sp, ch 1, rep from * around, join with sl st in first dc.

SKIRT

Rnd 1 (right side):

Fold Waistband lengthwise over drawstring so that Rnd 1 is behind Rnd 5 and ends of drawstring are threaded through Rnd 2 of adjacent sps on opposite side of Waistband, ch 1; working through both thicknesses of Rnd 5 and Rnd 1, (sc in next sp, ch 1) around, join with sl st in beg sc.

NOTE: Loop a short piece of thread around any stitch to mark Rnd 1 as right side.

Rnd 2:

Ch 3 (**counts as first dc, now and throughout**), sk next ch-1 sp and next sc, (2 dc, ch 2, 2 dc) in next ch-1 sp, sk next sc and next ch-1 sp, * dc in next sc, sk next ch-1 sp and next sc, (2 dc, ch 2, 2 dc) in next ch-1 sp, sk next sc and next ch-1 sp, rep from * around, join with sl st in first dc: {39-42}{45-48-51} ch-2 sps.

Rnds 3-6:

Ch 3, sk next 2 dc, (2 dc, ch 2, 2 dc) in next ch-2 sp, * sk next 2 dc, dc in next dc, sk next 2 dc, (2 dc, ch 2, 2 dc) in next ch-2 sp, rep from * around, join with sl st in first dc.

Rnd 7:

Ch 5, sk next 2 dc, sc in next ch-2 sp, ch 3, sk next 2 dc, * hdc in next dc, ch 3, sk next 2 dc, sc in next ch-2 sp, ch 3, sk next 2 dc, rep from * around, join with sl st in second ch of beg ch-5.

Rnd 8:

Sl st in first ch-3 sp changing to Red (**Fig. 4, page 95**), ch 2, 2dctog in same sp, ch 2, (3dctog in next ch-3 sp, ch 2) around, join with sl st in top of beg 2dctog changing to Yellow.

Rnd 9:
Ch 5, hdc in same st, [(hdc, ch 3, hdc) in next 3dctog] around, join with sl st in second ch of beg ch-5.

Rnd 10:
Sl st in first ch-3 sp changing to Black, ch 2, 2dctog in same sp, ch 2, (3dctog in next ch-3 sp, ch 2) around, join with sl st in top of beg 2dctog changing to Yellow.

Rnd 11:
Rep Rnd 9.

Rnd 12:
Sl st in first ch-3 sp changing to Red, ch 2, 2dctog in same sp, (ch 2, 3dctog in next sp) around, join with hdc in top of 2dctog changing to Black.

Rnd 13:
Ch 1, sc in last sp made, ch 3, (sc in next ch-2 sp, ch 3) around, join with sl st in beg sc. Fasten off.

FIRST MOTIF (make 1)
With Red, ch 6, join with sl st to form ring.

Rnd 1:
Ch 1, 12 sc in ring, join with sl st in front loop of first sc *(Fig. 1, page 95)*.

Rnd 2:
Working in front loop only, ch 1, sc in first st, ch 4, (sc in next 2 sc, ch 4) 5 times, sc in last sc, join with sl st in beg sc.

Rnd 3:
Work [(sl st, ch 2, 2 dc, ch 1, 2 dc, ch 2, sl st) in next ch-4 sp, ch 1] around, join with sl st in beg sl st, fasten off: 6 Petals.

Rnd 4:
Working **behind** Rnd 3 and in free loops of sts on Rnd 2 *(Fig. 3a, page 95)*, join Yellow with sl st in second sc, * † (ch 6, sc in fourth ch from hook, sl st in rem 2 chs, sl st in center of sc - Petal2 made), ch 2 †, sk next sc, sl st in next sc, rep from * 4 times **more**, then rep from † to † once, join with sl st in beg sl st. Fasten off.

Rnd 5:
Join Black with sc in ch-1 sp of any Petal on Rnd 3 *(see Joining with Sc, page 95)*, ch 4, sc in same sp, † ch 3, sc in tip of next Petal2, ch 3, sc in ch-1 sp of next Petal on Rnd 3, ch 3, (sc, ch 4, sc) in tip of next Petal2, ch 3, sc in ch-1 sp of next Petal on Rnd 3, ch 3, sc in tip of next Petal2 †, ch 3, (sc, ch 4, sc) in ch-1 sp of next Petal on Rnd 3, rep from † to † once, join with dc in beg sc.

Rnd 6:
Ch 1, sc in last sp made, ch 3, * † (3 dc, ch 2, 3 dc) in next ch-4 sp †, (ch 3, sc in next ch-3 sp) 3 times, ch 3, rep from * 2 times **more**, then rep from † to † once, (ch 3, sc in next sp) twice, join with dc in beg sc.

Rnd 7:

Ch 1, sc in last sp made, ch 3, sc in next ch-3 sp, ch 3, (2 hdc, ch 3, 2 hdc) in next ch-2 sp, (ch 3, sc in next ch-3 sp) 4 times, ch 3, 2 hdc in next ch-2 sp, ch 1, with **right** side of Skirt facing and Rnd 13 closest to you, sl st in second ch of last ch-3 sp of Rnd 13 of **Skirt**, ch 1, 2 hdc in same sp of **Motif**, (ch 1, sl st in second ch of next ch-3 sp of Rnd 13 of **Skirt**, ch 1, sc in next ch-3 sp of **Motif**) 4 times, ch 1, sl st in second ch of next ch-3 sp of Rnd 13 of **Skirt**, ch 1, 2 hdc in next ch-2 sp of **Motif**, ch 1, sl st in second ch of next ch-3 sp of Rnd 13 of **Skirt**, ch 1, 2 hdc in same ch-2 sp of **Motif**, (ch 3, sc in next sp) 4 times, ch 3, (2 hdc, ch 3, 2 hdc) in next ch-2 sp, (ch 3, sc in next sp) twice, ch 3, join with sl st in beg sc. Fasten off.

MIDDLE MOTIF
(make {11-12}{13-14-15})
Rnds 1-6:
Work same as Rnds 1-6 of First Motif.

Rnd 7:

Placing new Motif to the left of previous Motif, ch 1, sc in last sp made, ch 3, sc in next sp, ch 3, 2 hdc in next ch-2 sp, ch 1, sl st in second ch of corresponding ch-3 sp at lower left corner of **previous Motif**, ch 1, 2 hdc in same ch-2 sp of **new Motif**, (ch 1, sl st in second ch of next ch-3 sp of **previous Motif**, ch 1, sc in next ch-3 sp of **new Motif**) 4 times, ch 1, sl st in second ch of next ch-3 sp of **previous Motif**, ch 1, 2 hdc in next ch-2 sp of **new Motif**, ch 1, sl st in same st of Rnd 13 of **Skirt** as last joining sl st made, ch 1, 2 hdc in same sp of **new Motif**, (ch 1, sl st in second ch of next ch-3 sp of Rnd 13 of **Skirt**, ch 1, sc in next ch-3 sp of **new Motif**) 4 times, ch 1, sl st in second ch of next ch-3 sp of Rnd 13 of **Skirt**, ch 1,

2 hdc in next ch-2 sp of **new Motif**, ch 1, sl st in second ch of next ch-3 sp of Rnd 13 of **Skirt**, ch 1, 2 hdc in same ch-2 sp of **new Motif**, (ch 3, sc in next sp) 4 times, ch 3, (2 hdc, ch 3, 2 hdc) in next ch-2 sp, (ch 3, sc in next sp) twice, ch 3, join with sl st in beg sc. Fasten off.

LAST MOTIF (make 1)
Rnds 1-6:
Work same as Rnds 1-6 of First Motif.

Rnd 7:

Placing new Motif to the left of previous Motif, ch 1, sc in last sp made, ch 3, sc in next sp, ch 3, 2 hdc in next ch-2 sp, ch 1, sl st in second ch of corresponding ch-3 sp at lower left corner of **previous Motif**, ch 1, 2 hdc in same ch-2 sp of **new Motif**, (ch 1, sl st in second ch of next ch-3 sp of **previous Motif**, ch 1, sc in next ch-3 sp of **new Motif**) 4 times, ch 1, sl st in second ch of next ch-3 sp of **previous Motif**, ch 1, 2 hdc in next ch-2 sp of **new Motif**, ch 1, sl st in same st of Rnd 13 of **Skirt** as last joining sl st made, ch 1, 2 hdc in same sp of **new Motif**, (ch 1, sl st in second ch of next ch-3 sp of Rnd 13 of **Skirt**, ch 1, sc in next ch-3 sp of **new Motif**) 4 times, ch 1, sl st in second ch of next ch-3 sp of Rnd 13 of **Skirt**, ch 1, 2 hdc in next ch-2 sp of **new Motif**, ch 1, sl st in same st of Rnd 13 of Skirt as first joining st made, ch 1, 2 hdc in same ch-2 sp of **new Motif**, (ch 1, sl st in second ch of next ch-3 sp of **First Motif**, ch 1, sc in next ch-3 sp of **new Motif**) 4 times, ch 1, sl st in second ch of next ch-3 sp of **First Motif**, ch 1, 2 hdc in next ch-2 sp of new Motif, ch 1, sl st in second ch of next ch-3 sp of **First Motif**, ch 1, 2 hdc in same ch-2 sp of **new Motif**, (ch 3, sc in next ch-3 sp of **new Motif**) twice, ch 3, join with sl st in beg sc. Fasten off.

SKIRT SECTION 2

Rnd 1:
With **right** side facing, join Red with sc in joining between First and Last Motifs, *† [ch 1, (dc, ch 1) 3 times in second ch of next ch-3 sp, sc in second ch of next ch-3 sp] twice, ch 1, (dc, ch 1) 3 times in second ch of next ch-3 sp †, sc in joining between next 2 Motifs, rep from * {11-12} {13-14-15} times **more**, then rep from † to † once, join with sl st in beg sc, changing to Yellow.

Rnd 2:
Ch 2, dc in next dc, ch 3, sc in next dc, ch 3, * [(sk next ch, YO, pull up a loop in next st, YO, pull through 2 loops on hook) 3 times, YO, pull through all loops on hook], ch 3, sc in next dc, ch 3, rep from * around to last dc, dc in last dc, join with sl st in first dc changing to Black.

Rnd 3:
Ch 1, sc in same st, ch 1, sk next ch-3 sp, (dc, ch 1) 3 times in next sc, sk next ch-3 sp, * sc in next st, ch 1, sk next ch-3 sp, (dc, ch 1) 3 times in next sc, sk next ch-3 sp, rep from * around, join with sl st in beg sc.

Rnd 4:
Rep Rnd 2, changing to Red.

Rnd 5:
Rep Rnd 3, changing to Yellow.

Rnds 6-8:
Rep Rnds 2-4.

Rnd 9:
Ch 1, sc in same st, ch 3, sc in next sp, ch 3, sc in next sc, ch 3, sc in next sp, * ch 3, sc in next st, ch 3, sc in next sp, ch 3, sc in next sc, ch 3, sc in next sp, rep from * around, join with dc in beg sc: {156-168}{180-192-204} ch-3 sps.

Rnd 10:
Ch 1, sc in last sp made, ch 3, (sc in next sp, ch 3) around, join with sl st in beg sc.

Rnd 11:
Sl st in next sp, ch 3, (2 dc, ch 2, 2 dc) in next sp, * dc in next sp, (2 dc, ch 2, 2 dc) in next sp, rep from * around, join with sl st in first dc.

Rnds 12-18:
Ch 3, sk next 2 dc, (2 dc, ch 2, 2 dc) in next ch-2 sp, * sk next 2 dc, dc in next dc, sk next 2 dc, (2 dc, ch 2, 2 dc) in next ch-2 sp, rep from * around, join with sl st in first dc.

Rnd 19:
Ch 5, sk next 2 dc, sc in next ch-2 sp, ch 3, sk next 2 dc, * hdc in next dc, ch 3, sk next 2 dc, sc in next ch-2 sp, ch 3, sk next 2 dc, rep from * around, join with sl st in second ch of beg ch-5.

Rnd 20:
Sl st in first ch-3 sp changing to Red, ch 2, 2dctog in same sp, ch 2, (3dctog in next ch-3 sp, ch 2) around, join with sl st in top of beg 2dctog changing to Yellow.

Rnd 21:
Ch 5, hdc in same st, [(hdc, ch 3, hdc) in next 3dctog] around, join with sl st in second ch of beg ch-5.

Rnd 22:
Sl st in first ch-3 sp changing to Black, ch 2, 2dctog in same sp, ch 2, (3dctog in next ch-3 sp, ch 2) around, join with sl st in top of beg 2dctog changing to Yellow.

Rnd 23:
Rep Rnd 21.

Rnd 24:

Sl st in first ch-3 sp changing to Red, ch 2, 2dctog in same sp, (ch 2, 3dctog in next sp) around, join with hdc in top of beg 2dctog changing to Black.

Rnd 25:

Ch 1, sc in last sp made, ch 3, (sc in next ch-2 sp, ch 3) around, join with sl st in beg sc. Fasten off.

FIRST MOTIF2 (make 1)

Follow instructions for First Motif connecting First Motif2 to Rnd 25 of Skirt Section 2.

MIDDLE MOTIF2
(make {24-26}{28-30-32})

Follow instructions for Middle Motif connecting motifs to Rnd 25 of Skirt Section 2.

LAST MOTIF2 (make 1)

Follow instructions for Last Motif connecting Last Motif2 to Rnd 25 of Skirt Section 2.

SKIRT SECTION 3
Rnds 1-18:

Rep Rnds 1-18 of Skirt Section 2.

Rnd 19:

Ch 3, sk next 2 dc, (2 dc, ch 2, hdc in top of dc just made, 2 dc) in next ch-2 sp, * sk next 2 dc, dc in next dc, sk next 2 dc, (2 dc, ch 2, hdc in top of dc just made, 2 dc) in next ch-2 sp, rep from * around, join with sl st in first dc. Fasten off.

Dancer's delight

Whether you glide to a waltz or step lively to a salsa, this feminine skirt set will showcase your every move. The button-closure yoked skirt can be made to sit at your waist or your hip, while the scalloped hem of the sleeveless top picks up the rhythm of the skirt's ruffle. No dance floor in sight? Just enjoy the music this sweeping ensemble will inspire in your imagination. And you can make the music last by wearing the top and skirt with other separates in your wardrobe.

top

FINISHED CHEST SIZE:

X-Small	33$^1/_4$" (84.5 cm)	Large	40$^3/_8$" (102.5 cm)
Small	35$^5/_8$" (90.5 cm)	X-Large	42$^3/_4$" (108.5 cm)
Medium	38" (96.5 cm)		

Instructions are written with sizes X-Small and Small in the first set of braces
{ } and with sizes Medium, Large, and X-Large in the second set of braces.
Instructions will be easier to read if you circle all the numbers pertaining to
your size. If only one number is given, it applies to all sizes.

MATERIALS
Bedspread Weight Cotton Thread (size 10)
   [350 yards (320 meters) per ball]:
      {3-4}{4-4-5} balls
Steel crochet hook, size 7 (1.65 mm)
   or size needed for gauge
$^7/_{16}$" (11 mm) Buttons: {9-9}{9-10-10}
Sewing needle and matching thread

GAUGE:
Working in pattern:
   4 Shells = 2$^3/_8$" (6 cm)
   8 rows = 2" (5 cm)

SPECIAL STITCHES:
Hdc in center of sc just made or hdc in top of dc just made: YO, insert
hook through one horizontal bar and one vertical bar of specified stitch
(Fig. 5, page 95), YO, pull up a loop, YO, pull through all loops on hook.

Shell: (Dc, ch 2, dc) in next sc, sc in next sp.

BODY

Top is worked in one piece to armholes.

Ch {338-362}{386-410-434}.

Row 1 (right side):
Sc in second ch from hook, * sk next 2 chs, (dc, ch 2, dc) in next ch, sk next 2 chs, sc in next ch, rep from * across: {56-60}{64-68-72} ch-2 sps.

NOTE: Loop a short piece of thread around any stitch to mark Row 1 as **right** side.

Row 2:
Ch 4 (**counts as first dc plus ch 1, now and throughout**), turn; dc in same st, sc in next sp, work Shell, ch 4, skip next 2 sts, sc in next sp, * work 3 Shells, ch 4, skip next 2 sts, sc in next sp, rep from * {12-13} {14-15-16} times **more**, work Shell, (dc, ch 1, dc) in last sc: {57-61} {65-69-73} sps.

Row 3:
Ch 1, turn; sc in first st, work Shell, (ch 4, sc in next sp) twice, * work 2 Shells, (ch 4, sc in next sp) twice, rep from * {12-13}{14-15-16} times **more**, work Shell ending with sc in last dc: {56-60}{64-68-72} sps.

Row 4:
Ch 4, turn; dc in same st, sc in next sp, (ch 4, sc in next sp) 3 times, * work Shell, (ch 4, sc in next sp) 3 times, rep from * {12-13}{14-15-16} times **more**, (dc, ch 1, dc) in last sc: {57-61}{65-69-73} sps.

Row 5:
Rep Row 3.

Row 6:
Rep Row 2.

Row 7:
Ch 1, turn; sc in first st, work Shells across ending with sc in last dc.

Row 8:
Rep Row 2.

Row 9:
Rep Row 3.

Row 10:
Rep Row 2.

Row 11:
Rep Row 7.

Row 12:
Rep Row 2.

Row 13:
Rep Row 7.

Row 14:
Rep Row 2.

Row 15:
Rep Row 7.

Row 16:
Ch 4, turn; dc in same st, sc in next sp, work Shells across to last sc, (dc, ch 1, dc) in last sc.

Rep Rows 15 and 16, {14-14} {15-15-16} times.

NOTE: Bottom border will add an additional 3" (7.5 cm) of length.

ARMHOLE SHAPING

Ch 1, turn; sc in first st, work {13-13}{14-15-15} Shells, [(hdc, ch 1, hdc) in next sc, sc in next sp] {2-4}{4-4-6} times, work {26-26}{28-30-30} Shells, [(hdc, ch 1, hdc) in next sc, sc in next sp] {2-4}{4-4-6} times, work {13-13}{14-15-15} Shells.

RIGHT BACK

Row 1:
Ch 4, turn; dc in same st, sc in next sp, work {12-12}{13-14-14} Shells, leave remaining sts unworked.

Row 2:
Turn; sk first sc, sl st in next dc, ch 1, sc in next sp, work {12-12}{13-14-14} Shells ending with sc in last dc.

Row 3:
Ch 4, turn; dc in same st, sc in next sp, work {11-11}{12-13-13} Shells, dc in last sc.

Row 4:
Ch 4, turn; dc in same st, sc in next sp, work {11-11}{12-13-13} Shells ending with sc in last dc.

Row 5:
Ch 4, turn; dc in same st, sc in next sp, work {11-11}{12-13-13} Shells ending with sc in last dc.

Rows 6 thru {17-17}{17-19-19}:
Ch 4, turn; dc in same st, sc in next sp, work {11-11}{12-13-13} Shells ending with sc in last dc.

NECK SHAPING

Ch 4, turn; dc in same st, sc in next sp, work {8-8}{9-9-9} Shells, (dc, ch 2, hdc) in next sc, sc in next sp, [(hdc, ch 1, hdc) in next sc, sc in next sp] {2-2}{2-3-3} times ending with sc in last dc. Fasten off.

RIGHT BACK STRAP

Row 1:
With **wrong** side facing, sk first {2-2}{2-3-3} sps and join thread with sl st in next sp, ch 3, sc in next sp, work {8-8}{9-9-9} Shells ending with sc in last dc.

Row 2:
Ch 4, turn; dc in same st, sc in next sp, work {7-7}{8-8-8} Shells.

Row 3:
Turn; sk first sc, sl st in next dc, ch 1, sc in next sp, work {7-7}{8-8-8} Shells ending with sc in last dc.

Row 4:
Ch 4, turn; dc in same st, sc in next sp, work {6-6}{7-7-7} Shells.

Row 5:
Turn; sk first sc, sl st in next dc, ch 1, sc in next sp, work {6-6}{7-7-7} Shells ending with sc in last dc.

Row 6:
Ch 4, turn; dc in same st, sc in next sp, work {5-5}{6-6-6} Shells, dc in last sc.

Row 7:
Ch 3 (**counts as first dc**), turn; dc in same st, sc in next sp, work {5-5}{6-6-6} Shells ending with sc in last dc.

Row 8:
Ch 4, turn; dc in same st, sc in next sp, work {5-5}{6-6-6} Shells ending with sc in last dc.

Row 9:
Ch 3, turn; sc in next sp, work {5-5}{6-6-6} Shells ending with sc in last dc.

Row 10:
Ch 4, turn; dc in same st, sc in next sp, work {4-4}{5-5-5} Shells, 2 dc in last dc.

Row 11:
Ch 1, turn; sc in first st, work {5-5} {6-6-6} Shells ending with sc in last dc.

Row 12:
Ch 4, turn; dc in same st, sc in next sp, work {4-4}{5-5-5} Shells, (dc, ch 1, dc) in last sc.

Rep Rows 11 and 12, {1-1}{2-2-3} time(s).

Finishing Row:
Ch 1, turn; sc in first st, * (hdc, ch 1, hdc) in sc, sc in next sp, rep from * across ending with sc in last dc. Fasten off.

FRONT
Row 1:
With **wrong** side facing, join thread with sc in next ch-2 sp of Armhole Shaping row *(see Joining with Sc, page 95)*, work {25-25}{27-29-29} Shells, leave remaining sts unworked.

Row 2:
Turn; sl st in first dc, ch 1, sc in next sp, work {24-24}{26-28-28} Shells.

Row 3:
Ch 3, turn; sc in next sp, work {23-23}{25-27-27} Shells, dc in last dc.

Row 4:
Ch 3, turn; dc in same st, sc in next sp, work {22-22}{24-26-26} Shells, 2 dc in last dc.

Row 5:
Ch 1, turn; sc in first st, work {23-23}{25-27-27} Shells ending with sc in last dc.

Row 6:
Ch 4, turn; dc in same st, sc in next sp, work {22-22}{24-26-26} Shells, (dc, ch 1, dc) in last dc.

Row 7:
Ch 1, turn; sc in first st, work {23-23}{25-27-27} Shells ending with sc in last dc.

Rep Rows 6 and 7, {1-1}{1-2-2} time(s).

NECK SHAPING
Ch 4, turn; dc in same st, sc in next sp, work {8-8}{9-9-9} Shells, (dc, ch 2, hdc) in next sc, sc in next sp, [(hdc, ch 1, hdc) in next sc, sc in next sp] {4-4}{4-6-6} times, (hdc, ch 2, dc) in next sc, sc in next sp, work {8-8} {9-9-9} Shells, (dc, ch 1, dc) in last sc.

RIGHT FRONT STRAP
Row 1:
Ch 1, turn; sc in first st, work {8-8} {9-9-9} Shells, dc in next dc, leave remaining sts unworked.

Row 2:
Turn; sl st in first dc, ch 1, sc in next sp, work {7-7}{8-8-8} Shells, (dc, ch 1, dc) in last sc.

Row 3:
Ch 1, turn; sc in first st, work {7-7} {8-8-8} Shells.

Row 4:
Turn; sl st in first dc, ch 1, sc in next sp, work {6-6}{7-7-7} Shells, (dc, ch 1, dc) in last sc.

Row 5:
Ch 1, turn; sc in first st, work {6-6} {7-7-7} Shells, dc in last sc.

Row 6:
Ch 3, turn; dc in same st, sc in next sp, work {5-5}{6-6-6} Shells, (dc, ch 1, dc) in last sc.

Row 7:
Ch 1, turn; sc in first st, work {6-6} {7-7-7} Shells ending with sc in last dc.

Row 8:
Ch 3, turn; sc in next sp, work {5-5} {6-6-6} Shells, (dc, ch 1, dc) in last sc.

Row 9:
Ch 1, turn; sc in first st, work {5-5} {6-6-6} Shells, 2 dc in last dc.

Row 10:
Ch 1, turn; sc in first st, work {5-5} {6-6-6} Shells, (dc, ch 1, dc) in last sc.

Row 11:
Ch 1, turn; sc in first st, work {5-5} {6-6-6} Shells, dc in last sc.

Row 12:
Ch 3, turn; dc in same st, sc in next sp, work {4-4}{5-5-5} Shells, (dc, ch 1, dc) in last sc.

Row 13:
Ch 1, turn; sc in first st, work {5-5} {6-6-6} Shells ending with sc in last dc.

Row 14:
Ch 4, turn; dc in same st, sc in next sp, work {4-4}{5-5-5} Shells, (dc, ch 1, dc) in last sc.

Row 15:
Ch 1, turn; sc in first st, work {5-5} {6-6-6} Shells ending with sc in last dc.

Rep Rows 14 and 15, {3-3}{4-4-5} times, then rep Row 14 once **more**.

Finishing Row:
Ch 1, turn; sc in first st, * (hdc, ch 1, hdc) in next sc, sc in next sp, rep from * across ending with sc in last dc. Fasten off.

LEFT FRONT STRAP

Row 1:
With **wrong** side facing, sk next ch-2 sp of Neck Shaping row and join thread with sl st in next dc, ch 3, sc in next sp, work {8-8}{9-9-9} Shells ending with sc in last dc.

Row 2:
Ch 4, turn; dc in same st, sc in next sp, work {7-7}{8-8-8} Shells.

Row 3:
Turn; sl st in first dc, ch 1, sc in next sp, work {7-7}{8-8-8} Shells ending with sc in last dc.

Row 4:
Ch 4, turn; dc in same st, sc in next sp, work {6-6}{7-7-7} Shells.

Row 5:
Ch 3, turn; sc in next sp, work {6-6} {7-7-7} Shells ending with sc in last dc.

Row 6:
Ch 4, turn; dc in same st, sc in next sp, work {5-5}{6-6-6} Shells, 2 dc in last dc.

Row 7:
Ch 1, turn; sc in first st, work {6-6} {7-7-7} Shells ending with sc in last dc.

Row 8:
Ch 4, turn; dc in same st, sc in next sp, work {5-5}{6-6-6} Shells, dc in last sc.

Row 9:
Ch 3, turn; dc in same st, sc in next sp, work {5-5}{6-6-6} Shells ending with sc in last dc.

Row 10:
Ch 4, turn; dc in same st, sc in next sp, work {5-5}{6-6-6} Shells ending with sc in last dc.

Row 11:
Ch 3, turn; sc in next sp, work {5-5}{6-6-6} Shells ending with sc in last dc.

Row 12:
Ch 4, turn; dc in same st, sc in next sp, work {4-4}{5-5-5} Shells, 2 dc in last dc.

Row 13:
Ch 1, turn; sc in first st, work {5-5} {6-6-6} Shells ending with sc in last dc.

Row 14:
Ch 4, turn; dc in same st, sc in next sp, work {4-4}{5-5-5} Shells, (dc, ch 1, dc) in last sc.

Rep Rows 13 and 14, {4-4}{5-5-6} times.

Finishing Row:
Ch 1, turn; sc in first st, * (hdc, ch 1, hdc) in next sc, sc in next sp, rep from * across ending with sc in last dc. Fasten off.

LEFT BACK
Row 1:
With **wrong** side facing, join thread with sc in next ch-2 sp of Armhole Shaping row, work {12-12}{13-14-14} Shells, (dc, ch 1, dc) in last sc.

Row 2:
Ch 1, turn; sc in first st, work {12-12}{13-14-14} Shells.

Row 3:
Ch 3, turn; sc in next sp, work {11-11}{12-13-13} Shells, (dc, ch 1, dc) in last sc.

Row 4:
Ch 1, turn; sc in first st, work {11-11} {12-13-13} Shells, 2 dc in last dc.

Rows 5 thru {17-17}{17-19-19}:
Ch 1, turn; sc in first st, work {11-11} {12-13-13} Shells, (dc, ch 1, dc) in last sc.

NECK SHAPING
Ch 1, turn; sc in first st, [(hdc, ch 1, hdc) in next sc, sc in next sp] {2-2} {2-3-3} times, (hdc, ch 2, dc) in next sc, sc in next sp, work {8-8}{9-9-9} Shells, (dc, ch 1, dc) in last sc.

LEFT BACK STRAP
Row 1:
Ch 1, turn; sc in first st, work {8-8} {9-9-9} Shells, sk next 2 sts, dc in next dc, leave remaining sts unworked.

Row 2:
Turn; sl st in first dc, ch 1, sc in next sp, work {7-7}{8-8-8} Shells, (dc, ch 1, dc) in last sc.

Row 3:
Ch 1, turn; sc in first st, work {7-7} {8-8-8} Shells.

Row 4:
Turn; sl st in first dc, ch 1, sc in next sp, work {6-6}{7-7-7} Shells, (dc, ch 1, dc) in last sc.

Row 5:
Ch 1, turn; sc in first st, work {6-6} {7-7-7} Shells.

Row 6:
Ch 3, turn; sc in next sp, work {5-5}{6-6-6} Shells, (dc, ch 1, dc) in last sc.

Row 7:
Ch 1, turn; sc in first st, work {5-5}{6-6-6} Shells, 2 dc in last dc.

Row 8:
Ch 1, turn; sc in first st, work {5-5}{6-6-6} Shells, (dc, ch 1, dc) in last sc.

Row 9:
Ch 1, turn; sc in first st, work {5-5}{6-6-6} Shells, dc in last sc.

Row 10:
Ch 3, turn; dc in same st, sc in next sp, work {4-4}{5-5-5} Shells, (dc, ch 1, dc) in last sc.

Row 11:
Ch 1, turn; sc in first st, work {5-5}{6-6-6} Shells ending with sc in last dc.

Row 12:
Ch 4, turn; dc in same st, sc in next sp, work {4-4}{5-5-5} Shells, (dc, ch 1, dc) in last sc.

Row 13:
Ch 1, turn; sc in first st, work {5-5}{6-6-6} Shells ending with sc in last dc.

Rep Rows 12 and 13, {0-0}{1-1-2} time(s) (*see Zeros, page 95*), then rep Row 12 once **more**.

Finishing Row:
Ch 1, turn; sc in first st, * (hdc, ch 1, hdc) in next sc, sc in next sp, rep from * across ending with sc in last dc. Fasten off.

Sew straps together along top edge.

BOTTOM BORDER

Row 1:
With **wrong** side facing and working in free loops of beginning ch (*Fig. 3b, page 95*), join thread with sl st in ch at base of first sc, ch 4, dc in same st, sk next 2 chs, sc in next ch, sk next 2 chs, (dc, ch 2, dc) in next ch, sk next 2 chs, sc in next ch, ch 4, sk next 5 chs, sc in next ch, * [sk next 2 chs, (dc, ch 2, dc) in next ch, sk next 2 chs, sc in next ch] 3 times, ch 4, sk next 5 chs, sc in next ch, rep from * {12-13}{14-15-16} times **more**, sk next 2 chs, (dc, ch 2, dc) in next ch, sk next 2 chs, sc in next ch, sk next 2 chs, (dc, ch 1, dc) in last ch.

Row 2:
Ch 1, turn; sc in first st, work Shell, (ch 4, sc in next sp) twice, * work 2 Shells, (ch 4, sc in next sp) twice, rep from * {12-13}{14-15-16} times **more**, work Shell ending with sc in last dc.

Row 3:
Ch 4, turn; dc in same st, sc in next sp, ch 4, sc in next sp, * work Shell, ch 4, sc in next sp, rep from * across to last sc, (dc, ch 1, dc) in last sc.

Row 4:
Ch 1, turn; sc in first st, ch 4, sc in next sp, work 2 Shells, * (ch 4, sc in next sp) twice, work 2 Shells, rep from * across to last dc, ch 4, sc in last dc.

Row 5:
Ch 5 (**counts as first dc plus ch 2, now and throughout**), turn; sc in next sp, work Shell, * ch 4, sc in next sp, work Shell, rep from * across to last sc, ch 2, dc in last sc.

Row 6:
Ch 1, turn; sc in first st, work Shell, (ch 4, sc in next sp) twice, * work 2 Shells, (ch 4, sc in next sp) twice, rep from * {12-13}{14-15-16} times **more**, work Shell ending with sc in last dc.

Row 7:
Ch 5, turn; sc in next sp, ch 4, sc in next sp, 5 dc in next sc, sc in next sp, * (ch 4, sc in next sp) 3 times, 5 dc in next sc, sc in next sp, rep from * {12-13}{14-15-16} times **more**, ch 4, sc in next sp, ch 2, dc in last sc.

Row 8:
Ch 1, turn; sc in first st, ch 4, sc in next sp, (ch 1, dc in next dc) 5 times, ch 1, sc in next sp, * (ch 4, sc in next sp) twice, (ch 1, dc in next dc) 5 times, ch 1, sc in next sp, rep from * {12-13}{14-15-16} times **more**, ch 4, sc in last dc.

Row 9:
Ch 5, turn; sc in next sp, ch 1, dc in next dc, ch 1, [(dc, ch 1) twice in next dc] 3 times, dc in next dc, ch 1, sc in next ch-4 sp, * ch 4, sc in next ch-4 sp, ch 1, dc in next dc, ch 1, [(dc, ch 1) twice in next dc] 3 times, dc in next dc, ch 1, sc in next ch-4 sp, rep from * {12-13}{14-15-16} times **more**, ch 2, dc in last sc.

Row 10:
Ch 1, turn; sc in first st, * dc in next dc, (ch 2, hdc in top of dc just made, dc in next dc) 3 times, ch 2, hdc in top of dc just made, dc in next ch-1 sp, (ch 2, hdc in top of dc just made, dc in next dc) 4 times, sc in next ch-4 sp, rep from * across ending with sc in last dc. Fasten off.

RIGHT BACK BORDER
Row 1 (Button Row):
With **right** side facing, and working along side of Right Back, join thread with sc around sc at top edge, * 2 sc around dc at end of next row, sc around sc at end of next row, rep from * {33-33}{33-37-37} times **more**, ending with sc around sc at end of Row {6-6}{4-10-8} of Bottom Border: {103-103}{103-115-115} sc.

Row 2:
Ch 1, turn; sc in each sc across. Fasten off.

LEFT BACK BORDER
Row 1:
With **right** side facing, and working along side of Left Back, join thread with sc around sc at end of Row {6-6}{4-10-8} of Bottom Border, * 2 sc around dc at end of next row, sc around sc at end of next row, rep from * {33-33}{33-37-37} times **more**: {103-103}{103-115-115} sc.

Row 2 (Buttonhole Row):
Ch 1, turn; sc in first 2 sc, (ch 2, sk next 2 sc, sc in next 4 sc) {16-16} {16-18-18} times, ch 2, sk next 2 sc, sc in last 3 sc.

Row 3:
Ch 1, turn; sk first sc, sc in next sc, *† ch 1, [(dc, ch 2, hdc in top of dc just made) twice, dc] in next ch-2 sp, ch 1, sk next sc †, sc in next 2 sc, sk next sc, ch 1, rep from * {15-15} {15-17-17} times **more**, then rep from † to † once, sc in last sc of side, ch 2, hdc in center of sc just made, sc in same st as last sc made, [ch 2, hdc in center of sc just made, sc in next st or sp approx ¼" (0.5 cm) from previous sc] around neck edge ending with sc in sc at top right edge, ch 2, hdc in center of sc just made, sc in same st as last sc made, (ch 2, hdc in center of sc just made, sk next sc, sc in next sc) {51-51}{51-57-57} times. Fasten off.

Sew buttons to Row 1 of Right Back Border to correspond with every other ch-2 sp of Row 2 of Left Back Border beg with first ch-2 sp.

ARMHOLE BORDER

With **right** side facing, join thread with sc at center point of bottom of Armhole, ch 2, hdc in center of sc just made, * sc in next st or sp approx ¼" (0.5 cm) away from previous sc, ch 2, hdc in center of sc just made, rep from * around armhole edge, join with sl st in beg sc. Fasten off.

Rep for second Armhole.

skirt

FINISHED WAIST SIZE:

X-Small: 24$\frac{1}{4}$" (61.5 cm)   Large: 29$\frac{3}{8}$" (74.5 cm)
Small: 26" (66 cm)   X-Large: 31" (78.5 cm)
Medium: 27$\frac{5}{8}$" (69.5 cm)

FINISHED LENGTH:

X-Small, Small and Medium: 30" (76 cm)
Large and X-Large: 31$\frac{1}{2}$" (80 cm)

Instructions are written with sizes X-Small and Small in the first set of braces {} and with sizes Medium, Large, and X-Large in the second set of braces. Instructions will be easier to read if you circle all the numbers pertaining to your size. If only one number is given, it applies to all sizes.

OPTION: Directions are written for a skirt that sits at the waistline; to create a skirt that sits on the hip, follow directions for a larger skirt, adjusting the length as desired.

MATERIALS

Bedspread Weight Cotton Thread (size 10)
    [1000 yards (914 meters) per ball]:
    {3-4}{4-5-5} balls
Steel crochet hook, size 7 (1.65 mm)
    or size needed for gauge
$\frac{7}{16}$" (11 mm) Buttons: {7-7}{7-8-8}
Sewing needle and matching thread
Lightweight material for lining
Skirt pattern for lining (Butterick #3134 used for model)

GAUGE:

Working in rows of dc:
    7 dc = 1" (2.5 cm)
    4 rows = 1$\frac{1}{4}$" (3.25 cm)

SPECIAL STITCHES:

Hdc in center of sc just made or hdc in top of dc just made: YO, insert hook through one horizontal bar and one vertical bar of specified stitch *(Fig. 5, page 95)*, YO, pull up a loop, YO, pull through all loops on hook.

Dc in center of sc just made or dc in top of dc just made: YO, insert hook through one horizontal bar and one vertical bar of specified stitch *(Fig. 5, page 95)*, YO, pull up a loop, YO, pull through 2 loops on hook, YO, pull through rem loops on hook.

SKIRT
YOKE
Ch {176-188}{200-212-224}.

Row 1 (right side):
Dc in fifth ch from hook and in each ch across: {173-185}{197-209-221} sts.

NOTE: Loop a short piece of thread around any stitch to mark Row 1 as right side.

Row 2:
Ch 1, turn; sc in first st, * ch 4, sk next 3 dc, sc in next st, rep from * across: {43-46}{49-52-55} ch-4 sps.

Row 3:
Ch 4 (**counts as first dc plus ch 1, now and throughout**), turn; dc in same st, sc in next sp, * (dc, ch 2, dc) in next sc, sc in next sp, rep from * across to last sc, (dc, ch 1, dc) in last sc.

Row 4:
Ch 1, turn; sc in first st, * (dc, ch 2, dc) in next sc, sc in next sp, rep from * across ending with sc in last dc.

Row 5:
Rep Row 3.

Row 6:
Ch 1, turn; sc in same st, * (hdc, ch 1, hdc) in next sc, sc in next sp, rep from * across ending with sc in last dc.

Row 7 (inc row):
X-Small Only:
Ch 3 (**counts as first dc, now and throughout**), turn; 3 dc in next ch-1 sp, 2 dc in next sc, * 3 dc in next ch-1 sp, dc in next sc, 3 dc in next ch-1 sp, 2 dc in next sc, rep from * across: 195 dc.
Small Only:
Ch 3 (**counts as first dc, now and throughout**), turn; * 3 dc in next ch-1 sp, dc in next sc, 3 dc in next ch-1 sp, 2 dc in next sc, rep from * across to last 2 sps, (3 dc in next ch-1 sp, dc in next sc) twice: 207 dc.
Medium Only:
Ch 3 (**counts as first dc, now and throughout**), turn; 3 dc in next ch-1 sp, * dc in next sc, 3 dc in next ch-1 sp, 2 dc in next sc, 3 dc in next ch-1 sp, rep from * across to last sc, dc in last sc: 221 dc.

Large Only:
Ch 3 (**counts as first dc, now and throughout**), turn; * 3 dc in next ch-1 sp, dc in next sc, 3 dc in next ch-1 sp, 2 dc in next sc, rep from * across: 235 dc.
X-Large Only:
Ch 3 (**counts as first dc, now and throughout**), turn; 3 dc in next ch-1 sp, 2 dc in next sc, * 3 dc in next ch-1 sp, dc in next sc, 3 dc in next ch-1 sp, 2 dc in next sc, rep from * across: 249 dc.

Row 8:
Ch 1, turn; sc in first {2-2}{1-2-1} dc, * ch 4, sk next 3 dc, sc in next dc, rep from * across to last {5-5}{4-5-4} dc, ch 4, sk next 3 dc, sc in last {2-2}{1-2-1} dc: {48-51}{55-58-62} ch-4 sps.

Row 9:
X-Small, Small and Large Only:
Ch 3, turn; (dc, ch 1, dc) in next st, sc in next sp, * (dc, ch 2, dc) in next sc, sc in next sp, rep from * across to last ch-4 sp, (dc, ch 1, dc) in next sc, dc in last sc.

Row 9:

Medium and X-Large Only:

Ch 4, turn; dc in same st, sc in next sp, * (dc, ch 2, dc) in next sc, sc in next sp, rep from * across to last ch-4 sp, (dc, ch 1, dc) in last sc.

Row 10:

X-Small, Small and Large Only:

Ch 1, turn; sc in first st and in next ch-1 sp, * (dc, ch 2, dc) in next sc, sc in next sp, rep from * across to last dc, sc in last dc.

Medium and X-Large Only:

Ch 1, turn; sc in first st, * (dc, ch 2, dc) in next sc, sc in next sp, rep from * across ending with sc in last dc.

Row 11:

Rep Row 9.

Row 12:

X-Small, Small and Large Only:

Ch 1, turn; sc in first st and in next ch-1 sp, * (hdc, ch 1, hdc) in next sc, sc in next sp, rep from * across to last dc, sc in last dc.

Medium and X-Large Only:

Ch 1, turn; sc in first st, * (hdc, ch 1, hdc) in next sc, sc in next sp, rep from * across ending with sc in last dc.

Row 13 (inc row):

X-Small Only:

Ch 3, turn; sc in next st, * 3 dc in next ch-1 sp, dc in next sc, 3 dc in next ch-1 sp, 2 dc in next sc, rep from * across to last sc, dc in last sc: 219 dc.

Small Only:

Ch 3, turn; dc in next st, 3 dc in next ch-1 sp, 2 dc in next sc, * 3 dc in next ch-1 sp, dc in next sc, 3 dc in next ch-1 sp, 2 dc in next sc, rep from * across to last sc, dc in last sc: 233 dc.

Medium Only:

Ch 3, turn; 3 dc in next ch-1 sp, 2 dc in next sc, * 3 dc in next ch-1 sp, dc in next sc, 3 dc in next ch-1 sp, 2 dc in next sc, rep from * across: 249 dc.

Large Only:

Ch 3, turn; dc in next st, * 3 dc in next ch-1 sp, dc in next sc, 3 dc in next ch-1 sp, 2 dc in next sc, rep from * across to last 2 sps, (3 dc in next ch-1 sp, dc in next sc) twice, dc in last sc: 263 dc.

X-Large Only:

Ch 3, turn; * 3 dc in next ch-1 sp, dc in next sc, 3 dc in next ch-1 sp, 2 dc in next sc, rep from * across to last 2 sps, (3 dc in next ch-1 sp, dc in next sc) twice: 279 dc.

Row 14:

Ch 1, turn; sc in first {2-1}{1-2-2} dc, * ch 4, sk next 3 dc, sc in next dc, rep from * across to last {5-4}{4-5-5} dc, ch 4, sk next 3 dc, sc in last {2-1} {1-2-2} dc: {54-58}{62-65-69} ch-4 sps.

Row 15:

X-Small, Large and X-Large Only:

Ch 3, turn; (dc, ch 1, dc) in next st, sc in next sp, * (dc, ch 2, dc) in next sc, sc in next sp, rep from * across to last 2 sc, (dc, ch 1, dc) in next sc, dc in last sc.

Small and Medium Only:

Ch 4, turn; dc in same st, sc in next sp, * (dc, ch 2, dc) in next sc, sc in next sp, rep from * across to last sc, (dc, ch 1, dc) in last sc.

Row 16:

X-Small, Large and X-Large Only:

Ch 1, turn; sc in first st and in next ch-1 sp, * (dc, ch 2, dc) in next sc, sc in next sp, rep from * across to last dc, sc in last dc.

Row 16:
Small and Medium Only:
Ch 1, turn; sc in first st, * (dc, ch 2, dc) in next sc, sc in next sp, rep from * across ending with sc in last dc.

Row 17:
Rep Row 15.

Row 18:
X-Small, Large and X-Large Only:
Ch 1, turn; sc in first st and in next ch-1 sp, * (hdc, ch 1, hdc) in next sc, sc in next sp, rep from * across to last dc, sc in last dc.
Small and Medium Only:
Ch 1, turn; sc in first st, * (hdc, ch 1, hdc) in next sc, sc in next sp, rep from * across ending with sc in last dc.

Row 19 (inc row):
X-Small Only:
Ch 3, turn; dc in next st, * 3 dc in next ch-1 sp, dc in next sc, 3 dc in next ch-1 sp, 2 dc in next sc, rep from * across to last 2 sps, (3 dc in next ch-1 sp, dc in next sc) twice, dc in last sc: 245 dc.
Small Only:
Ch 3, turn; * 3 dc in next ch-1 sp, dc in next sc, 3 dc in next ch-1 sp, 2 dc in next sc, rep from * across to last 2 sps, (3 dc in next ch-1 sp, dc in next sc) twice: 261 dc.
Medium Only:
Ch 3, turn; * 3 dc in next ch-1 sp, dc in next sc, 3 dc in next ch-1 sp, 2 dc in next sc, rep from * across to last 2 sps, (3 dc in ch-1 sp, dc in sc) twice: 279 dc.
Large Only:
Ch 3, turn; dc in next st, * 3 dc in next ch-1 sp, dc in next sc, 3 dc in next ch-1 sp, 2 dc in next sc, rep from * across to last sp, 3 dc in next ch-1 sp, dc in next sc, dc in last sc: 295 dc.

X-Large Only:
Ch 3, turn; dc in next st, * 3 dc in next ch-1 sp, dc in next sc, 3 dc in next ch-1 sp, 2 dc in next sc, rep from * across to last sp, 3 dc in next ch-1 sp, dc in next sc, dc in last sc: 313 dc.

Row 20:
Ch 1, turn; sc in first {1-1}{2-2-1} dc, * ch 4, sk next 3 dc, sc in next dc, rep from * across to last {4-4}{5-5-4} dc, ch 4, sk next 3 dc, sc in last {1-1} {2-2-1} dc: {61-65}{69-73-78} ch-4 sps.

Row 21:
X-Small, Small and X-Large Only:
Ch 4, turn; dc in same st, sc in next sp, * (dc, ch 2, dc) in next sc, sc in next sp, rep from * across to last sc, (dc, ch 1, dc) in last sc.
Medium and Large Only:
Ch 3, turn; (dc, ch 1, dc) in next st, sc in next sp, * (dc, ch 2, dc) in next sc, sc in next sp, rep from * across to last 2 sc, (dc, ch 1, dc) in next sc, dc in last sc.

Row 22:
X-Small, Small and X-Large Only:
Ch 1, turn; sc in first st, * (dc, ch 2, dc) in next sc, sc in next sp, rep from * across ending with sc in last dc.
Medium and Large Only:
Ch 1, turn; sc in first st and in next ch-1 sp, * (dc, ch 2, dc) in next sc, sc in next sp, rep from * across to last dc, sc in last dc.

Row 23:
Rep Row 21.

Row 24:

X-Small, Small and X-Large Only:
Ch 1, turn; sc in first st, * (hdc, ch 1, hdc) in next sc, sc in next sp, rep from * across ending with sc in last dc.

Medium and Large Only:
Ch 1, turn; sc in first st and in next ch-1 sp, * (hdc, ch 1, hdc) in next sc, sc in next sp, rep from * across to last dc, sc in last dc.

Row 25 (inc row):

X-Small Only:
Ch 3, turn; dc in same st, 3 dc in next ch-1 sp, * dc in next sc, 3 dc in next ch-1 sp, 2 dc in next sc, 3 dc in next ch-1 sp, rep from * across to last sc, 2 dc in last sc, do **not** fasten off: 277 dc.

Skip to Skirt Yoke Ruffle.

Small Only:
Ch 3, turn; 3 dc in next ch-1 sp, 2 dc in next sc, (3 dc in next ch-1 sp, dc in next sc) twice, * 3 dc in next ch-1 sp, 2 dc in next sc, 3 dc in next ch-1 sp, dc in next sc, rep from * across to last 2 sps, (3 dc in next ch-1 sp, dc in next sc) twice, do **not** fasten off: 292 dc.

Skip to Skirt Yoke Ruffle.

Medium Only:
Ch 3, turn; 2 dc in next st, 3 dc in next ch-1 sp, 2 dc in next sc, 3 dc in next ch-1 sp, dc in next sc, * (3 dc in next ch-1 sp, 2 dc in next sc) 3 times, (3 dc in next ch-1 sp, dc in next sc) twice, rep from * across to last 2 sps, (3 dc in next ch-1 sp, 2 dc in next sc) twice, dc in last sc, do **not** fasten off: 322 dc.

Skip to Skirt Yoke Ruffle.

Large Only:
Ch 3, turn; dc in next st, 3 dc in next ch-1 sp, * dc in next sc, 3 dc in next ch-1 sp, 2 dc in next sc, 3 dc in next ch-1 sp, rep from * across to last 2 sc, dc in last 2 sc: 331 dc.

X-Large Only:
Ch 3, turn; * 3 dc in next ch-1 sp, dc in next sc, 3 dc in next ch-1 sp, 2 dc in next sc, rep from * across to last 2 sps, (3 dc in next ch-1 sp, dc in next sc) twice: 351 dc.

Row 26:

Large and X-Large Only:
Ch 1, turn; sc in first 2 dc, * ch 4, sk next 3 dc, sc in next dc, rep from * across to last 5 dc, ch 4, sk next 3 dc, sc in last 2 dc: {82-87} ch-4 sps.

Row 27:

Large and X-Large Only:
Ch 3, turn; (dc, ch 1, dc) in next st, sc in next sp, * (dc, ch 2, dc) in next sc, sc in next sp, rep from * across to last 2 sc, (dc, ch 1, dc) in next sc, dc in last sc.

Row 28:

Large and X-Large Only:
Ch 1, turn; sc in first st, sc in next ch-1 sp, * (dc, ch 2, dc) in next sc, sc in next sp, rep from * across to last dc, sc in last dc.

Row 29:

Large and X-Large Only:
Rep Row 27.

Row 30:

Large and X-Large Only:
Ch 1, turn; sc in first st and in next ch-1 sp, * (hdc, ch 1, hdc) in next sc, sc in next sp, rep from * across to last dc, sc in last dc.

Row 31 (inc row):
Large Only:
Ch 3, turn; dc in next st, (3 dc in next ch-1 sp, dc in next sc) 5 times, * 3 dc in next ch-1 sp, dc in next sc, 3 dc in next ch-1 sp, 2 dc in next sc, rep from * across to last 5 sps, (3 dc in next ch-1 sp, dc in next sc) 5 times, dc in last sc: 367 dc.

Row 31 (inc row):
X-Large Only:
Ch 3, turn; 2 dc in next st, (3 dc in next ch-1 sp, 2 dc in next sc) twice, 3 dc in next ch-1 sp, * dc in next sc, 3 dc in next ch-1 sp, 2 dc in next sc, 3 dc in next ch-1 sp, rep from * across to last 2 sc, 2 dc in next sc, dc in last sc: 397 dc.

SKIRT YOKE RUFFLE
Row 1:
Ch 1, turn; sc in first st, * ch 3, sk next 2 sts, sc in next st, rep from * across: {92-97}{107-122-132} ch-3 sps.

Row 2:
Ch 4, turn; sc in next sp, (ch 3, sc in next sp) twice, ch 1, 5 dc in next sp, ch 1, sc in next sp, * (ch 3, sc in next sp) 3 times, ch 1, 5 dc in next sp, ch 1, sc in next sp, rep from * across to last 2 sps, (ch 3, sc in next sp) twice, ch 1, dc in last sc.

Row 3:
Ch 1, turn; sc in first st, * sk next ch-1 sp, (ch 3, sc in next ch-3 sp) twice, ch 1, (dc in next dc, ch 1) twice, (dc, ch 1) twice in next dc, (dc in next dc, ch 1) twice, sk next ch-1 sp, sc in next ch-3 sp, rep from * across to last 2 sps, ch 3, sc in next ch-3 sp, ch 3, sk next ch-1 sp, sc in last dc.

Row 4:
Turn; sk first sc, sl st in next sp, ch 1, sc in same sp, ch 3, dc in center of sc just made, sc in next sp, *sk next sc, dc in next dc, (ch 3, dc in top of dc just made, dc in next dc) 5 times, sk next ch-1 sp, sc in next ch-3 sp, ch 3, dc in center of sc just made, sc in next ch-3 sp, rep from * across, sl st in last sc. Fasten off.

LOWER SKIRT
Row 1:
With **right** side facing, join thread with sl st in first dc of last row of Skirt Yoke (same st as first sc on Row 1 of Ruffle), ch 5 (**counts as first dc plus ch 2, now and throughout**), working **behind** Ruffle and in skipped sts on last row of Skirt Yoke, hdc in next skipped st, * ch 3, hdc in next skipped st, rep from * across, ch 2, dc in same st as last sc on Row 1 of Ruffle: {185-195}{215-245-265} sps.

Row 2:
Ch 1, turn; sc in first st, * ch 4, sc in next sp, rep from * across ending with sc in last dc.

Row 3:
Ch 5, turn; sc in next sp, ch 4, sc in next sp, (dc, ch 2, dc) in next sc, sc in next sp, * (ch 4, sc in next sp) 4 times, (dc, ch 2, dc) in next sc, sc in next sp, rep from * across to last sp, ch 4, sc in last sp, ch 2, dc in last sc.

Row 4:
Ch 1, turn; sc in first st, ch 4, sc in next sp, [(dc, ch 2, dc) in next sc, sc in next sp] twice, * ch 4, sc in next sp, (dc, ch 2, dc) in next sc, sc in next sp, ch 4, sc in next sp, [(dc, ch 2, dc) in next sc, sc in next sp] twice, rep from * across to last dc, ch 4, sc in last dc.

Row 5:
Turn; sk first sc, sc in first sp, * ch 4, sc in next sp, rep from * across to last sc, ch 2, dc in last sc.

Row 6:
Ch 1, turn; sc in first st, (ch 4, sc in next sp) 4 times, * (dc, ch 2, dc) in next sc, sc in next sp, (ch 4, sc in next sp) 4 times, rep from * across ending with sc in last dc.

Row 7:
Ch 4, turn; dc in next sc, sc in next sp, ch 4, sc in next sp, (dc, ch 2, dc) in next sc, sc in next sp, ch 4, sc in next sp, * [(dc, ch 2, dc) in next sc, sc in next sp] twice, ch 4, sc in next sp, (dc, ch 2, dc) in next sc, sc in next sp, ch 4, sc in next sp, rep from * across to last sc, (dc, ch 1, dc) in last sc.

Row 8:
Ch 1, turn; sc in first st, (ch 4, sc in next sp) across ending with sc in last dc.

Rows 9-74:
Rep Rows 3-8, 11 times **or** until desired length, ending by working Row 8.

Rows 75 and 76:
Rep Rows 3 and 4 once **more**.

Row 77:
Ch 1, turn; sc in first sp, (dc, ch 2, dc) in next sc, sc in next sp, ch 4, sc in next sp, (dc, ch 2, dc) in next sc, sc in next sp, * (ch 4, sc in next sp) twice, (dc, ch 2, dc) in next sc, sc in next sp, ch 4, sc in next sp, (dc, ch 2, dc) in next sc, sc in next sp, rep from * across to last sc, ch 2, dc in last sc.

Row 78:
Ch 1, turn; sc in first st, (dc, ch 2, dc) in next sc, sc in next sp, (ch 4, sc in next sp) twice, (dc, ch 2, dc) in next sc, sc in next sp, * ch 4, sc in next sp, (dc, ch 2, dc) in next sc, sc in next sp, (ch 4, sc in next sp) twice, (dc, ch 2, dc) in next sc, sc in next sp, rep from * across ending with sc in last dc.

Row 79:
Ch 5, turn; sc in first sp, ch 4, sc in next sp, 5 dc in next sc, * sc in next sp, (ch 4, sc in next sp) 4 times, 5 dc in next sc, rep from * across to last 2 sps, (ch 4, sc in next sp) twice, ch 2, dc in last sc.

Row 80:

Ch 1, turn; sc in first st, ch 4, sc in next sp, (ch 1, dc in next dc) 5 times, ch 1, sc in next sp, * (ch 4, sc in next sp) 3 times, (ch 1, dc in next dc) 5 times, ch 1, sc in next sp, rep from * across to last dc, ch 4, sc in last dc.

Row 81:

Ch 5, turn; sc in first sp, ch 1, dc in next dc, [(ch 1, dc) twice in next dc] 3 times, ch 1, dc in next dc, ch 1, sc in next ch-4 sp, * (ch 4, sc in next sp) twice, ch 1, dc in next dc, [(ch 1, dc) twice in next dc] 3 times, ch 1, dc in next dc, ch 1, sc in next ch-4 sp, rep from * across to last sc, ch 2, dc in last sc.

Row 82:

Ch 1, turn; sc in first st, ch 1, (dc in next dc, ch 2) 7 times, dc in next dc, ch 1, sc in next ch-4 sp, * ch 4, sc in next ch-4 sp, ch 1, (dc in next dc, ch 2) 7 times, dc in next dc, ch 1, sc in next ch-4 sp, rep from * across ending with sc in last dc.

Row 83:

Ch 2, turn; * (dc in next dc, ch 2, hdc in top of dc just made) 4 times, dc in next ch-2 sp, ch 2, hdc in top of dc just made, (dc in next dc, ch 2, hdc in top of dc just made) 4 times, sc in next ch-4 sp, ch 2, hdc in center of sc just made, rep from * {35-37}{41-47-51} times **more**, (dc in next dc, ch 2, hdc in top of dc just made) 4 times, dc in next ch-2 sp, ch 2, hdc in top of dc just made, (dc in next dc, ch 2, hdc in top of dc just made) 3 times, (YO, insert hook in **next** st, YO, pull up a loop, YO, pull through 2 loops on hook) twice, YO, pull through all loops on hook. Fasten off.

Sew Lower Skirt together at back, leaving Skirt Yoke open.

BUTTONHOLE BORDER
Row 1:

With **right** side facing, join thread with sc around dc at bottom edge of left side of Skirt Yoke back *(see Joining with Sc, page 95)*, sc around same dc, (sc around sc at end of next row, 2 sc around dc at end of next row) {12-12}{12-15-15} times; working in free loops of beginning ch *(Fig. 3b, page 95)*, 3 sc in ch at base of first dc, sc in next {171-183}{195-207-219} chs, 3 sc in last ch; working along edge of right side of Skirt Yoke back, 2 sc around dc at end of first row, (sc around sc at end of next row, 2 sc around dc at end of next row) {12-12}{12-15-15} times.

Row 2:

X-Small, Small, and Medium Only:

Ch 1, turn; sc in first 39 sc along side, 3 sc in next sc, sc in next {173-185}{197} sc, 3 sc in next sc, (ch 2, sk next 2 sc, sc in next 4 sc) 6 times, ch 2, sk next 2 sc, sc in last sc.

NOTE: Ch-2 sps create buttonholes.

Large and X-Large Only:

Ch 1, turn; sc in first 48 sc along side, 3 sc in next sc, sc in next {209-221} sc, 3 sc in next sc, sc in next sc, (ch 2, sk next 2 sc, sc in next 4 sc) 7 times, ch 2, sk next 2 sc, sc in last 3 sc.

NOTE: Ch-2 sps create buttonholes.

Row 3:

X-Small, Small, and Medium Only:

Ch 1, turn; sc in first st, *† ch 1, dc in next ch-2 sp, (ch 2, hdc in top of dc just made, dc in same sp) twice †, ch 1, sk next sc, sc in next 2 sc, sk next sc, rep from * 5 times **more**, then rep from † to † once, ch 1, sk next sc, sc in next sc, (ch 2, sc in center of sc just made, sk next sc, sc in next sc) {88-94}{100} times, ch 3, sc in same st as last sc made, (ch 2, sc in center of sc just made, sk next sc, sc in next sc) 20 times. Fasten off.

Large and X-Large Only:

Ch 1, turn; sc in first 2 sts, sk next st, *† ch 1, dc in next ch-2 sp, (ch 2, hdc in top of dc just made, dc in same sp) twice †, ch 1, sk next sc, sc in next 2 sc, sk next sc, rep from * 6 times **more**, then rep from † to † once, ch 1, sk next sc, sc in next 2 sc, ch 3, sc in same st as last sc made, (ch 2, sc in center of sc just made, sk next sc, sc in next sc) {106-112} times, ch 3, sc in same st as last sc made, (ch 2, sc in center of sc just made, sk next sc, sc in next sc) 24 times, sl st in last sc. Fasten off.

FINISHING

Sew buttons to Row 1 of left side of Skirt Yoke to correspond with buttonholes on right side.

Garden of dreams

Sometimes the simplicity of a single blossom makes it more beautiful than an entire bouquet. And if less is truly more, then this top-and-skirt pair has it all. The knee-length skirt is easy-on with a button closure, while the tapered shoulders of the lacy top only hint at the idea of sleeves. Each piece pairs well with other garments, so an entire garden of fashion can branch out from this one amazing skirt set.

top

FINISHED CHEST SIZE:

X-Small:	$32\frac{1}{2}$" (82.5 cm)		Large:	41" (104 cm)
Small:	36" (91.5 cm)		X-Large:	$44\frac{1}{2}$" (113 cm)
Medium:	$39\frac{1}{4}$" (99.5 cm)			

Instructions are written with sizes X-Small and Small in the first set of braces { } and with sizes Medium, Large, and X-Large in the second set of braces. Instructions will be easier to read if you circle all the numbers pertaining to your size. If only one number is given, it applies to all sizes.

MATERIALS

Bedspread Weight Cotton Thread (size 10) [350 yards (320 meters) per ball]: {4-4}{5-5-6} balls
Steel crochet hook, size 7 (1.65 mm) **or** size needed for gauge
$\frac{1}{2}$" (13 mm) Buttons: {9-9}{9-10-10-10}
Sewing needle and matching thread

GAUGE:

Motif measures 3" (7.5 cm) square.

SPECIAL STITCHES:

2dctog: (YO, insert hook in specified st, YO, pull up a loop, YO, pull through 2 loops on hook) twice, YO, pull through all loops on hook.

3dctog: (YO, insert hook in specified st, YO, pull up a loop, YO, pull through 2 loops on hook) 3 times, YO, pull through all loops on hook.

5dctog: (YO, insert hook in specified st, YO, pull up a loop, YO, pull through 2 loops on hook) 5 times, YO, pull through all loops on hook.

6dctog: (YO, insert hook in specified st, YO, pull up a loop, YO, pull through 2 loops on hook) 6 times, YO, pull through all loops on hook.

Tr: YO twice, insert hook in st or sp indicated, YO and pull up a loop, (YO, pull through 2 loops on hook) 3 times.

Sc in center of sc just made: Insert hook through one horizontal bar and one vertical bar of specified stitch *(Fig. 5, page 95)*, YO, pull up a loop, YO, pull through all loops on hook.

TOP
MOTIF BAND
FIRST MOTIF (make 1)
Ch 6, join with sl st to form ring.

Rnd 1 (right side):
Ch 1, (sc in ring, ch 2, tr in ring, ch 2, sc in ring, ch 5) 3 times, sc in ring, ch 2, tr in ring, ch 2, sc in ring, ch 1, join with tr in beg sc to form last sp: 12 sps.

NOTE: Loop a short piece of thread around any stitch to mark Rnd 1 as **right** side.

Rnd 2:
Ch 1, (sc, ch 3) twice in last sp made, [(sc, ch 3) twice in next tr, sk next ch-2 sp, (sc, ch 3) twice in next ch-5 sp] around to last tr, (sc, ch 3, sc) in last tr, join with dc in beg sc to form last sp: 16 ch-3 sps.

Rnd 3:
Ch 1, sc in last sp made, ch 1, 5 dc in next sp, ch 1, sc in next sp, [(ch 3, sc in next sp) twice, ch 1, 5 dc in next sp, ch 1, sc in next sp] 3 times, ch 3, sc in next sp, join with dc in beg sc to form last sp: 20 dc, 12 sc, and 16 sps.

Rnd 4:
Ch 1, sc in last sp made, *† (ch 1, dc in next dc) twice, ch 1, (dc, ch 1) twice in next dc, (dc in next dc, ch 1) twice, skip next ch-1 sp, sc in next ch-3 sp †, ch 3, sc in next ch-3 sp, rep from * 2 times **more**, then rep from † to † once, join with dc in beg sc to form last sp.

Rnd 5:
Ch 1, sc in last sp made, *† ch 3, sc in next ch-1 sp, ch 3, sk next dc and next ch-1 sp, sc in next dc, ch 3, sk next ch-1 sp and next dc, (hdc, ch 5, hdc) in next ch-1 sp, ch 3, sk next dc and next ch-1 sp, sc in next dc, ch 3, sk next ch-1 sp and next dc, sc in next ch-1 sp, ch 3 †, sc in next ch-3 sp, rep from * 2 times **more**, then rep from † to † once, join with sl st in beg sc. Fasten off.

JOINING MOTIF
(make {10-11}{12-13-14})
Rnds 1-4:
Work same as Rnds 1-4 of First Motif.

Rnd 5:
Placing Joining Motif to the left of previous Motif, ch 1, sc in last sp made, ch 3, sc in next ch-1 sp, ch 3, sk next dc and next ch-1 sp, sc in next dc, ch 3, sk next ch-1 sp and next dc, hdc in next ch-1 sp, ch 2, sl st in third ch of corresponding ch-5 sp of **previous Motif**, ch 2, hdc in same ch-1 sp of **new Motif**, † ch 1, sl st in second ch of next ch-3 sp of **previous Motif**, ch 1, sk next dc and next ch-1 sp of **new Motif**, sc in next dc, ch 1, sl st in second ch of next ch-3 sp of **previous Motif**, ch 1, sk next ch-1 sp and next dc of **new Motif** †, sc in next ch-1 sp, ch 1, sl st in second ch of next ch-3 sp of **previous Motif**, ch 1, sc in next ch-3 sp of **new Motif**, ch 1, sl st in second ch of next ch-3 sp of **previous Motif**, ch 1, sc in next ch-1 sp of **new Motif**, repeat from † to † once, hdc in next ch-1 sp, ch 2, sl st in third ch of next ch-5 sp of **previous Motif**, ch 2, hdc in same ch-1 sp of **new Motif**, * ch 3, sk next dc and next ch-1 sp, sc in next dc, ch 3, sk next ch-1 sp and next dc, sc in next ch-1 sp, ch 3, sc in next ch-3 sp, ch 3, sc in next ch-1 sp, ch 3, sk next dc and next ch-1 sp, sc in next dc, ch 3, sk next ch-1 sp and next dc, (hdc, ch 5, hdc) in next ch-1 sp, rep from * once **more**, ch 3, sk next dc and next ch-1 sp, sc in next dc, ch 3, sk next ch-1 sp and next dc, sc in last ch-1 sp, ch 3, join with sl st in beg sc. Fasten off.

BODY
Row 1:
With **wrong** side facing and working along top edge of Motif Band, join thread with sc in third ch of ch-5 sp at top right edge *(see Joining with Sc, page 95)*, (ch 3, sc in next ch-3 sp) 6 times, * ch 3, sc in joining between Motifs, (ch 3, sc in next ch-3 sp) 6 times, rep from * {9-10}{11-12-13} times **more**, ch 3, sc in third ch of ch-5 sp of last Motif: {77-84}{91-98-105} ch-3 sps.

Row 2:
X-Small Only:
Ch 1, turn; sc in first sc, (3 sc in next ch-3 sp) 18 times, 2 sc in next ch-3 sp, * (3 sc in next ch-3 sp) 19 times, 2 sc in next ch-3 sp, rep from * once **more**, (3 sc in next ch-3 sp) 17 times, 2 sc in next ch-3 sp, sc in last sc: 229 sc.

Small Only:
Ch 1, turn; sc in first sc, 2 sc in next ch-3 sp, 3 sc in each ch-3 sp across, sc in last sc: 253 sc.

Medium Only:
Ch 1, turn; sc in first sc, 2 sc in next ch-3 sp, (3 sc in next ch-3 sp) 21 times, * 4 sc in next ch-3 sp, (3 sc in next ch-3 sp) 22 times, rep from * 2 times **more**, sc in last sc: 277 sc.

Large Only:
Ch 1, turn; sc in first sc, * 2 sc in next ch-3 sp, (3 sc in next ch-3 sp) 13 times, rep from * 6 times **more**, sc in last sc: 289 sc.

X-Large Only:
Ch 1, turn; sc in first sc, 2 sc in next ch-3 sp, (3 sc in next ch-3 sp) 24 times, 2 sc in next ch-3 sp, * (3 sc in next ch-3 sp) 26 times, 2 sc in next ch-3 sp, rep from * once **more**, (3 sc in next ch-3 sp) 25 times, sc in last sc: 313 sc.

Row 3:
Ch 1, turn; sc in each sc across.

Row 4:
Ch 3 (**counts as first dc, now and throughout**), turn; 2 dc in same st, (sk next 2 sc, sc in next sc, sk next 2 sc, 5 dc in next sc) {37-41}{45-47-51} times, sk next 2 sc, sc in next sc, sk next 2 sc, 3 dc in last sc.

Row 5:
Ch 1, turn; sc in first st, (ch 2, 5dctog over next 5 sts, ch 2, sc in next st) {38-42}{46-48-52} times.

Row 6:
Ch 1, turn; sc in first st, (2 sc in next ch-2 sp, sc in next 5dctog, 2 sc in next ch-2 sp, sc in next st) {38-42} {46-48-52} times.

Row 7:
Ch 1, turn; sc in each sc across.

Rep Rows 4-7, {7-7}{7-8-8} times, do **not** fasten off.

FRONT
Row 1:
Ch 3, turn; 2 dc in same sc, (sk next 2 sc, sc in next sc, sk next 2 sc, 5 dc in next sc) {18-20}{22-23-25} times, sk next 2 sc, sc in next sc, sk next 2 sc, 3 dc in next sc, mark last dc made for beg of Back.

Row 2:
Ch 1, turn; sc in first st, (ch 2, 5dctog over next 5 sts, ch 2, sc in next st) {19-21}{23-24-26} times.

Row 3:
Ch 1, turn; sc in first st, (2 sc in next ch-2 sp, sc in next 5dctog, 2 sc in next ch-2 sp, sc in next sc) {19-21}{23-24-26} times: {115-127} {139-145-157} sc.

Row 4:
Ch 1, turn; sc in each sc across.

Rep Rows 1-4, 5 times, do **not** fasten off.

LEFT FRONT NECK
Row 1:
Ch 3, turn; 2 dc in same sc, (sk next 2 sc, sc in next sc, sk next 2 sc, 5 dc in next sc) {7-8}{8-8-9} times, sk next 2 sc, sc in next sc, leave rem sts unworked.

Row 2:
Turn; sk first sc, sl st in next 2 dc, ch 1, sc in next dc, (ch 2, 5dctog over next 5 sts, ch 2, sc in next dc) {7-8} {8-8-9} times.

Row 3:
Ch 1, turn; sc in first st, (2 sc in next ch-2 sp, sc in next 5dctog, 2 sc in next ch-2 sp, sc in next sc) {6-7}{7-7-8} times, 2 sc in next ch-2 sp, sc in next 5dctog, leave last sp and sc unworked: {40-46}{46-46-52} sc.

Row 4:
Ch 1, turn; sc in each sc across.

Row 5:
Ch 3, turn; 2 dc in same sc, (sk next 2 sc, sc in next sc, sk next 2 sc, 5 dc in next sc) {6-7}{7-7-8} times, sk next 2 sc, sc in last sc.

Row 6:
Turn; sk first sc, sl st in next 2 dc, ch 1, sc in next dc, (ch 2, 5dctog over next 5 sts, ch 2, sc in next dc) {6-7} {7-7-8} times.

Row 7:
Ch 1, turn; sc in first st, (2 sc in next ch-2 sp, sc in next 5dctog, sc in next ch-2 sp, sc in next sc) {5-6}{6-6-7} times, 2 sc in next ch-2 sp, sc in next 5dctog, leave last sp and sc unworked: {34-40}{40-40-46} sc.

Row 8:
Ch 1, turn; sc in each sc across.

Row 9:
Ch 3, turn; 2 dc in same sc, (sk next 2 sc, sc in next sc, sk next 2 sc, 5 dc in next sc) {5-6}{6-6-7} times, sk next 2 sc, sc in last sc.

Row 10:
Ch 2, turn; 2dctog over next 2 dc, ch 2, sc in next dc, (ch 2, 5dctog over next 5 sts, ch 2, sc in next dc) {5-6} {6-6-7} times.

Row 11:
Ch 1, turn; sc in first st, (2 sc in next ch-2 sp, sc in next 5dctog, 2 sc in next ch-2 sp, sc in next sc) {5-6}{6-6-7} times, 2 sc in next ch-2 sp, sc in next 2dctog, leave last ch-2 unworked: {34-40}{40-40-46} sc.

Row 12:
Ch 1, turn; sc in each sc across.

Rep Rows 9-12, {1-2}{2-2-3} time(s), then rep Rows 9-11 once **more**. Fasten off.

RIGHT FRONT NECK
Row 1:
With **right** side facing, sk next {23-23}{35-41-41} sc on last row of Front, join thread with sc in next sc, (sk next 2 sc, 5 dc in next sc, sk next 2 sc, sc in next sc) {7-8}{8-8-9} times, sk next 2 sc, 3 dc in last sc.

Row 2:
Ch 1, turn; sc in first st, (ch 2, 5dctog over next 5 sts, ch 2, sc in next dc) {6-7}{7-7-8} times, ch 2, 6dctog over last 6 sts.

Row 3:
Ch 1, turn; sc in first st, 2 sc in next ch-2 sp, sc in next sc, (2 sc in next sp, sc in next 5dctog, 2 sc in next ch-2 sp, sc in next sc) {6-7}{7-7-8} times: {40-46}{46-46-52} sc.

Row 4:
Ch 1, turn; sc in each sc across.

Row 5:
Ch 1, turn; sc in first st, (sk next 2 sc, 5 dc in next sc, sk next 2 sc, sc in next sc) {6-7}{7-7-8} times, sk next 2 sc, 3 dc in last sc.

Row 6:
Ch 1, turn; sc in first st, (ch 2, 5dctog over next 5 sts, ch 2, sc in next dc) {5-6}{6-6-7} times, ch 2, 6dctog over last 6 sts.

Row 7:
Ch 1, turn; sc in first st, 2 sc in next ch-2 sp, sc in next sc, (2 sc in next ch-2 sp, sc in next 5dctog, 2 sc in next ch-2 sp, sc in next sc) {5-6}{6-6-7} times: {34-40}{40-40-46} sc.

Row 8:
Ch 1, turn; sc in each sc across.

Row 9:
Ch 1, turn; sc in first st, (sk next 2 sc, 5 dc in next sc, sk next 2 sc, sc in next sc) {5-6}{6-6-7} times, sk next 2 sc, 3 dc in last sc.

Row 10:
Ch 1, turn; sc in first st, (ch 2, 5dctog over next 5 sts, ch 2, sc in next dc) {5-6}{6-6-7} times, ch 2, 3dctog over last 3 sts.

Row 11:
Ch 1, turn; sc in first st, 2 sc in next ch-2 sp, sc in next sc, (2 sc in next ch-2 sp, sc in next 5dctog, 2 sc in next ch-2 sp, sc in next sc) {5-6}{6-6-7} times: {34-40}{40-40-46} sc.

Row 12:
Ch 1, turn; sc in each sc across.

Rep Rows 9-12, {1-2}{2-2-3} time(s), then rep Rows 9-11 once **more**. Fasten off.

BACK
Row 1:
With **right** side facing, join thread with sl st in same st as marked dc of Row 1 of Front, ch 3, 2 dc in same st, sk next 2 sc, sc in next sc, (sk next 2 sc, 5 dc in next sc, sk next 2 sc, sc in next sc) {18-20}{22-23-25} times, sk next 2 sc, 3 dc in last sc.

Row 2:
Ch 1, turn; sc in first st, (ch 2, 5dctog over next 5 sts, ch 2, sc in next dc) {19-21}{23-24-26} times.

Row 3:
Ch 1, turn; sc in first st, (2 sc in next ch-2 sp, sc in next 5dctog, sc in next ch-2 sp, sc in next sc) {19-21}{23-24-26} times: {115-127}{139-145-157} sc.

Row 4:
Ch 1, turn; sc in each sc across.

Row 5:
Ch 3, turn; 2 dc in same sc, sk next 2 sc, sc in next sc, (sk next 2 sc, 5 dc in next sc, sk next 2 sc, sc in next sc) {18-20}{22-23-25} times, sk next 2 sc, 3 dc in last sc.

Rep Rows 2-5, {8-9}{9-9-10} times, then rep Rows 2-4 once **more**.

RIGHT SHOULDER
Row 1:
Ch 3, turn; 2 dc in same st, (sk next 2 sc, sc in next sc, sk next 2 sc, 5 dc in next sc) {6-7}{7-7-8} times, sk next 2 sc, sc in next sc, leave rem sts unworked.

Row 2:
Turn; sk first sc, sl st in next 2 dc, ch 1, sc in next dc, (ch 2, 5dctog over next 5 sts, ch 2, sc in next dc) {6-7}{7-7-8} times.

Row 3:
Ch 1, turn; sc in first st, 2 sc in next ch-2 sp, sc in next 5dctog, (2 sc in next ch-2 sp, sc in next sc, 2 sc in next ch-2 sp, sc in next 5dctog) {5-6}{6-6-7} times, leave last sp and sc unworked: {34-40}{40-40-46} sc. Fasten off.

LEFT SHOULDER
Row 1:
With **right** side facing, sk next {35-35}{47-53-53} sc on last row of Back, join thread with sc in next sc, (sk next 2 sc, 5 dc in next sc, sk next 2 sc, sc in next sc) {6-7}{7-7-8} times, sk next 2 sc, 3 dc in last sc.

Row 2:
Ch 1, turn; sc in first st, (ch 2, 5dctog over next 5 sts, ch 2, sc in next dc) {5-6}{6-6-7} times, ch 2, 6dctog over next 6 sts.

Row 3:
Ch 1, turn; sc in first st, 2 sc in next ch-2 sp, sc in next sc, (2 sc in next ch-2 sp, sc in next 5dctog, 2 sc in next ch-2 sp, sc in next sc) {5-6}{6-6-7} times: {34-40}{40-40-46} sc. Fasten off.

Sew shoulder seams.

BOTTOM BORDER

Row 1:
With **right** side facing and working along bottom edge of Motif Band, join thread with sc in third ch of ch-5 sp of first Motif, *† (ch 3, sc in next ch-3 sp) 3 times, (dc, ch 2, dc) in next sc, sc in next ch-3 sp, (ch 3, sc in next ch-3 sp) twice, ch 3 †, sc in joining between Motifs, rep from * {9-10}{11-12-13} times **more**, then rep from † to † once, sc in third ch of last ch-5 sp.

Row 2:
Ch 3, turn; dc in same st, sc in next ch-3 sp, *† (ch 3, sc in next ch-3 sp) twice, ch 1, 5 dc in next ch-2 sp, ch 1, sc in next ch-3 sp, (ch 3, sc in next ch-3 sp) twice †, (dc, ch 2, dc) in next sc, sc in next ch-3 sp, rep from * {9-10}{11-12-13} times **more**, then rep from † to † once, 2 dc in last sc.

Row 3:
Ch 3, turn; 2 dc in same st, ch 1, sc in next ch-3 sp, *† ch 3, sc in next ch-3 sp, ch 1, dc in next dc, [ch 1, (dc, ch 1, dc) in next dc, ch 1, dc in next dc] twice, ch 1, sc in next ch-3 sp, ch 3, sc in next ch-3 sp, ch 1 †, 5 dc in next ch-2 sp, ch 1, sc in next ch-3 sp, rep from * {9-10}{11-12-13} times **more**, then rep from † to † once, 3 dc in last dc.

Row 4:
Ch 4, turn; (dc, ch 1, dc) in next dc, ch 1, dc in next dc, ch 1, sc in next ch-3 sp, *† ch 1, dc in next dc, [ch 1, (dc, ch 1, dc) in next dc, ch 1, dc in next dc] 3 times, ch 1, sc in next ch-3 sp, ch 1, dc in next dc †, [ch 1, (dc, ch 1, dc) in next dc, ch 1, dc in next dc] twice, ch 1, sc in next ch-3 sp, rep from * {9-10}{11-12-13} times **more**, then rep from † to † once, ch 1,(dc, ch 1, dc) in next dc, ch 1, dc in last dc.

Row 5:
Ch 3, turn; sc in next ch-1 sp, (ch 3, sc in next ch-1 sp) twice, ch 3, (pull up a loop in next ch-1 sp) twice, YO, pull through all loops on hook, *† (ch 3, sc in next ch-1 sp) 9 times, ch 3, (pull up a loop in next ch-1 sp) twice, YO, pull through all loops on hook †, (ch 3, sc in next ch-1 sp) 6 times, ch 3, (pull up a loop in next ch-1 sp) twice, YO, pull through all loops on hook, rep from * {9-10} {11-12-13} times **more**, then rep from † to † once, (ch 3, sc in next ch-1 sp) twice, ch 3, sc in next ch-4 sp, ch 3, sl st in third ch of same ch 4.
Fasten off.

LEFT SIDE BORDER

Row 1:
With **right** side facing and working along side edge of Left Front, join thread with sc around dc at end of Row 4 of Bottom Border, sc around same st, (2 sc around dc at end of next row) twice, sc around sc at end of next row, (3 sc in next sp) 7 times, 2 sc in next sp, † (sc around sc at end of next row) 3 times, 2 sc around dc at end of next row †, rep from † to † {7-7} {7-8-8} times **more**, (sc around sc at end of next row) 3 times, sc around dc at end of next row, (ch 3, sc around sc at end of next row, ch 3, sk next 2 rows, sc around dc at end of next row) {10-11} {11-11-12} times, ch 3, sc around sc at end of next row, ch 3, sk next 2 rows (seamed rows), sc around sc at end of next row, (ch 3, sc around dc at end of next row, ch 3, sk next 2 rows, sc around sc at end of next row) {10-11}{11-11-12} times, ch 3, sc around dc at end of next row, rep from † to † {8-8}{8-9-9} times, (sc around sc at end of next row) 3 times, 2 sc in next sp, (3 sc in next sp) 7 times, sc around sc at end of next row, (2 sc around dc at end of next row) 3 times.

Row 2 (Buttonhole Row):
Ch 1, turn; sc in first {73-73} {73-78-78} sc, ch 1, sk next sc, sc in next ch-3 sp, * (ch 1, dc) 3 times in next ch-3 sp, ch 1, sc in next ch-3 sp, rep from * {20-22}{22-22-24} times **more**, ch 1, sk next sc, sc in next 2 sc, (ch 2, sk next 2 sc, sc in next 6 sc) {8-8}{8-9-9} times, ch 2, sk next 2 sc, sc in last {5-5}{5-2-2} sts.

Row 3:
Ch 1, turn; sc in first {1-1}{1-2-2} sc, (ch 2, sc in center of sc just made, sk next st, sc in next st) {2-2}{2-0-0} times *(see Zeros, page 95)*, * ch 2, sc in center of sc just made, sk next ch, sc in next ch, (ch 2, sc in center of sc just made, sk next st, sc in next st) 3 times, rep from * {7-7}{7-8-8} times **more**, ch 2, sc in center of sc just made, sk next ch, sc in next ch, ch 2, sc in center of sc just made, sk next sc, sc in next sc, † pull up a loop in each of next 2 sps, YO, pull through all loops on hook, (ch 3, sc in next sp) twice, ch 3 †, rep from † to † {20-22}{22-22-24} times **more**, pull up a loop in each of next 2 sps, YO, pull through all loops on hook, sc in next sc, (ch 2, sc in center of sc just made, sk next sc, sc in next sc) {36-36}{36-38-38} times, sc in last {0-0}{0-1-1} sc. Fasten off.

Sew buttons to Row 1 of Left Side Border to correspond with buttonholes along Front edge.

RIGHT ARMHOLE BORDER
Row 1:
With **right** side facing and working along side edge of Back, join thread with sc around first dc of Row 1 of Back, sc around same dc, ch 1, sc around sc at end of next row, (ch 3, sk next 2 rows, sc around dc at end of next row, ch 3, sc around sc at end of next row) {10-11}{11-11-12} times,

ch 3, sk next 2 rows (seamed rows), sc around sc at end of next row, (ch 3, sc around dc at end of next row, ch 3, sk next 2 rows, sc around sc at end of next row) {10-11} {11-11-12} times ch 1, 2 sc around dc at end of next row.

Row 2:
Ch 2, turn; sc in first sp, * (ch 1, dc) 3 times in next ch-3 sp, ch 1, sc in next sp, rep from * {20-22}{22-22-24} times **more**, sk next sc, hdc in last sc.

Row 3:
Turn; pull up a loop around first hdc, pull up a loop in next ch-1 sp, YO, pull through all loops on hook, * (ch 3, sc in next sp) twice, ch 3, pull up a loop in each of next 2 sps, YO, pull through all loops on hook, rep from * {20-22}{22-22-24} times **more**. Fasten off.

NECK BORDER
Rnd 1:
With **right** side facing and working along back neck edge, join thread with sc in first unworked st, (ch 1, sk next sc, sc in next sc) {17-17} {23-26-26} times, ch 1, sc around sc at end of next row, ch 1, sc in second dc of next 5-dc group, ch 1, sc around sixth dc of next 6dctog, ch 1, sc around sc of last row of Left Front, ch 1, sc around dc at end of next row, [(ch 1, sk next row, sc around sc at end of next row) twice, ch 1, sc around dc at end of next row] {2-3}{3-3-4} times, ch 1, sk next row, sc around sc at end of next row, (ch 1, sc in next 5dctog, ch 1, sc in next ch-2 sp, ch 1, sc in fourth dc of next 5-dc group, ch 1, sc around next sc) twice; working along center front neck edge, (ch 1, sk next sc, sc in next sc) {11-11}{17-20-20} times, (ch 1, sc around sc at end of next row, ch 1, sc in second dc of next 5-dc group, ch 1, sc around sixth dc of next 6dctog,

ch 1, sc around sc at end of next row) twice, (ch 1, sk next row, sc around sc at end of next row, ch 1, sc around dc at end of next row, ch 1, sk next row, sc around sc at end of next row) {3-4}{4-4-5} times, ch 1, sk seam, sc around sc at end of next row, ch 1, sc in next ch-2 sp, ch 1, sc in fourth dc of next 5-dc group, ch 1, sc around next sc, join with sc in beg sc.

Rnd 2:
Ch 1, sc in last sp made, ch 2, sc in center of sc just made, * sc in next ch-1 sp, ch 2, sc in center of sc just made, rep from * around, join with sl st in beg sc. Fasten off.

skirt

◼◼◼◻ INTERMEDIATE

FINISHED WAIST/HIP SIZE:
X-Small: 24"/35$\frac{1}{2}$" (61 cm/90 cm)
Small: 26$\frac{1}{4}$"/37$\frac{3}{4}$" (66.5 cm/96 cm)
Medium: 28$\frac{1}{2}$"/40" (72.5 cm/101.5 cm)

Large: 30$\frac{3}{4}$"/42" (78 cm/106.5 cm)
X-Large: 33"/44" (84 cm/112 cm)

Instructions are written with sizes X-Small and Small in the first set of braces { } and with sizes Medium, Large, and X-Large in the second set of braces. Instructions will be easier to read if you circle all the numbers pertaining to your size. If only one number is given, it applies to all sizes.

MATERIALS
Bedspread Weight Cotton Thread (size 10)
[350 yards (320 meters) per ball]:
{5-5}{6-6-6} balls
Steel crochet hook, size 7 (1.65 mm)
or size needed for gauge
$\frac{1}{2}$" (13 mm) buttons: 5
Sewing needle and matching thread
Lightweight material for lining
Skirt pattern for lining (Butterick #3134 used for model)

GAUGE:
Motif measures 3" (7.5 cm) square.

SPECIAL STITCHES:
5dctog: (YO, insert hook in specified st, YO, pull up a loop, YO, pull through 2 loops on hook) 5 times, YO, pull through all loops on hook.

2sctog: Pull up a loop in each of next 2 sts, YO, pull through all loops on hook.

Tr: YO twice, insert hook in st or sp indicated, YO and pull up a loop, (YO and pull through 2 loops on hook) 3 times.

Sc in center of sc just made: Insert hook through one horizontal bar and one vertical bar of specified stitch *(Fig. 5, page 95)*, YO, pull up a loop, YO, pull through all loops on hook.

SKIRT
LOWER SKIRT
FIRST MOTIF1 (make 1)
Ch 6, join with sl st to form ring.

Rnd 1:
Ch 1, (sc in ring, ch 2, tr in ring, ch 2, sc in ring, ch 5) 3 times, sc in ring, ch 2, tr in ring, ch 2, sc in ring, ch 1, join with tr in beg sc to form last sp: 12 sps.

Rnd 2:
Ch 1, (sc, ch 3) twice in last sp made, [(sc, ch 3) twice in next tr, (sc, ch 3) twice in next ch-5 sp] around to last tr, (sc, ch 3, sc) in last tr, join with dc in beg sc to form last sp: 16 ch-3 sps.

Rnd 3:
Ch 1, sc in last sp made, ch 1, 5 dc in next sp, ch 1, sc in next sp, [(ch 3, sc in next sp) twice, ch 1, 5 dc in next sp, ch 1, sc in next sp] 3 times, ch 3, sc in next sp, join with dc in beg sc to form last sp: 20 dc, 12 sc, and 16 sps.

Rnd 4:
Ch 1, sc in last sp made, *† (ch 1, dc in next dc) twice, ch 1, (dc, ch 1) twice in next dc, (dc in next dc, ch 1) twice, sc in next ch-3 sp †, ch 3, sc in next ch-3 sp, rep from * 2 times **more**, then rep from † to † once, join with dc in beg sc to form last sp.

Rnd 5:
Ch 1, sc in last sp made, *† ch 3, sc in next ch-1 sp, ch 3, sk next dc and next ch-1 sp, sc in next dc, ch 3, sk next ch-1 sp and next dc, (hdc, ch 5, hdc) in next ch-1 sp, ch 3, sk next dc and next ch-1 sp, sc in next dc, ch 3, sk next ch-1 sp and next dc, sc in next ch-1 sp, ch 3 †, sc in next ch-3 sp, rep from * 2 times **more**, then rep from † to † once, join with sl st in beg sc. Fasten off.

MIDDLE MOTIF1
(make {15-16} {17-18-19})
Rnds 1-4:
Work same as Rnds 1-4 of First Motif1.

Rnd 5:
Placing Middle Motif1 to the left of previous Motif, ch 1, sc in last sp made, ch 3, sc in next ch-1 sp, ch 3, sk next dc and next ch-1 sp, sc in next dc, ch 3, sk next ch-1 sp and next dc, hdc in next ch-1 sp, ch 2, sl st in third ch of corresponding ch-5 sp of **previous Motif**, ch 2, hdc in same ch-1 sp of **new Motif**, † ch 1, sl st in second ch of next ch-3 sp of **previous Motif**, ch 1, sk next dc and next ch-1 sp of **new Motif**, sc in next dc, ch 1, sl st in second ch of next ch-3 sp of **previous Motif**, ch 1, sk next ch-1 sp and next dc of **new Motif** †, sc in next ch-1 sp, ch 1, sl st in second ch of next ch-3 sp of **previous Motif**, ch 1, sc in next ch-3 sp of **new Motif**, ch 1, sl st in second ch of next ch-3 sp of **previous Motif**, ch 1, sc in next ch-1 sp of **new Motif**, repeat from † to † once, hdc in next ch-1 sp, ch 2, sl st in third ch of next ch-5 sp of **previous Motif**, ch 2, hdc in same ch-1 sp of **new Motif**, * ch 3, sk next dc and next ch-1 sp, sc in next dc, ch 3, sk next ch-1 sp and next dc, sc in next ch-1 sp, ch 3, sc in next ch-3 sp, ch 3, sc in next ch-1 sp, ch 3, sk next dc and next ch-1 sp, sc in next dc, ch 3, sk next ch-1 sp and next dc, (hdc, ch 5, hdc) in next ch-1 sp, rep from * once **more**, sc in next ch-3 sp, ch 3, sc in next ch-1 sp, ch 3, sk next ch-1 sp and next dc, sc in last ch-1 sp, ch 3, join with sl st in beg sc. Fasten off.

LAST MOTIF1 (make 1)
Rnds 1-4:
Work same as Rnds 1-4 of First Motif1.

Rnd 5:
Placing Last Motif1 to the left of previous Motif made, ch 1, sc in last sp made, ch 3, sc in next ch-1 sp, ch 3, sk next dc and next ch-1 sp, sc in next dc, ch 3, sk next ch-1 sp and next dc, † hdc in next ch-1 sp, ch 2, sl st in third ch of corresponding ch-5 sp of **previous Motif**, ch 2, hdc in same ch-1 sp of **new Motif**, ch 1, sl st in second ch of next ch-3 sp of **previous Motif**, ch 1, sk next dc and next ch-1 sp of **new Motif**, sc in next dc, ch 1, sl st in second ch of next ch-3 sp of **previous Motif**, ch 1, sk next ch-1 sp and next dc of **new Motif**, sc in next ch-1 sp, ch 1, sl st in second ch of next ch-3 sp of **previous Motif**, ch 1, sc in next ch-3 sp of **new Motif**, ch 1, sl st in second ch of next ch-3 sp of **previous Motif**, ch 1, sc in next ch-1 sp of **new Motif**, ch 1, sl st in second ch of next ch-3 sp of **previous Motif**, ch 1, sk next dc and next ch-1 sp of **new Motif**, sc in next dc, ch 1, sl st in second ch of next ch-3 sp of **previous Motif**, ch 1, sk next ch-1 sp and next dc of **new Motif**, hdc in next ch-1 sp, ch 2, sl st in third ch of ch-5 sp of **previous Motif**, ch 2, hdc in same ch-1 sp of **new Motif** †, ch 3, sk next dc and next ch-1 sp, sc in next dc, ch 3, sk next ch-1 sp and next dc, sc in next ch-1 sp, ch 3, sc in next ch-3 sp, ch 3, sc in next ch-1 sp, ch 3, sk next dc and next ch-1 sp, sc in next dc, ch 3, sk next ch-1 sp and next dc; connecting Last Motif1 to First Motif1, rep from † to † once, ch 3, sk next dc and next ch-1 sp, sc in next dc, ch 3, sk next ch-1 sp and next dc, sc in next ch-1 sp, ch 3, join with sl st in beg sc: circle of {17-18}{19-20-21} Motifs made. Fasten off.

FIRST MOTIF2 (make 1 per tier)
Rnds 1-4:
Work same as Rnds 1-4 of First Motif1.

Rnd 5:
Placing First Motif2 under any Motif on previous tier of Motifs, ch 1, sc in last sp made, ch 3, sc in next ch-1 sp, ch 3, sk next dc and next ch-1 sp, sc in next dc, ch 3, sk next ch-1 sp and next dc, (hdc, ch 5, hdc) in next ch-1 sp, ch 3, sk next dc and next ch-1 sp, sc in next dc, ch 3, sk next ch-1 sp and next dc, sc in next ch-1 sp, ch 3, sc in next ch-3 sp, ch 3, sc in next ch-1 sp, ch 3, sk next dc and next ch-1 sp, sc in next dc, ch 3, sk next ch-1 sp and next dc, hdc in next ch-1 sp, ch 2, sl st in third ch of corresponding ch-5 sp of **previous Motif**, ch 2, hdc in same ch-1 sp of **new Motif**, † ch 1, sl st in second ch of next ch-3 sp of **previous Motif**, ch 1, sk next dc and next ch-1 sp of **new Motif**, sc in next dc, ch 1, sl st in second ch of next ch-3 sp of **previous Motif**, ch 1, sk next ch-1 sp and next dc of **new Motif** †, sc in next ch-1 sp, ch 1, sl st in second ch of next ch-3 sp of **previous Motif**, ch 1, sc in next ch-3 sp of **new Motif**, ch 1, sl st in second ch of next ch-3 sp of **previous Motif**, ch 1, sc in next ch-1 sp of **new Motif**, repeat from † to † once, hdc in next ch-1 sp, ch 2, sl st in third ch of ch-5 sp of **previous Motif**, ch 2, hdc in same ch-1 sp of **new Motif**, ch 3, sk next dc and next ch-1 sp, sc in next dc, ch 3, sk next ch-1 sp and next dc, sc in next ch-1 sp, ch 3, sc in next ch-3 sp, ch 3, sc in next ch-1 sp, ch 3, sk next dc and next ch-1 sp, sc in next dc, ch 3, sk next ch-1 sp and next dc, (hdc, ch 5, hdc) in next ch-1 sp, ch 3, sk next dc and next ch-1 sp, sc in next dc, ch 3, sk next ch-1 sp and next dc, sc in next ch-1 sp, ch 3, join with sl st in beg sc. Fasten off.

MIDDLE MOTIF2
(make {15-16}{17-18-19} per tier)
Rnds 1-4:
Work same as Rnds 1-4 of First Motif1.

Rnd 5:
Placing Middle Motif2 to the left of previous Motif made, ch 1, sc in last sp made, ch 3, sc in next ch-1 sp, ch 3, sk next dc and next ch-1 sp, sc in next dc, ch 3, sk next ch-1 sp and next dc, * hdc in next ch-1 sp, ch 2, sl st in third ch of corresponding ch-5 sp of **previous Motif**, ch 2, hdc in same ch-1 sp of **new Motif**, † ch 1, sl st in second ch of next ch-3 sp of **previous Motif**, ch 1, sk next dc and next ch-1 sp of **new Motif** †, sc in next dc, ch 1, sl st in second ch of next ch-3 sp of **previous Motif**, ch 1, sk next ch-1 sp and next dc of **new Motif**, sc in next ch-1 sp, ch 1, sl st in second ch of next ch-3 sp of **previous Motif**, ch 1, sc in next ch-3 sp of **new Motif**, ch 1, sl st in second ch of next ch-3 sp of **previous Motif**, ch 1, sc in next ch-1 sp of **new Motif**, rep from † to † once, then rep from * once **more**, hdc in next ch-1 sp, ch 2, sl st in third ch of ch-5 sp of **previous Motif**, ch 2, hdc in same ch-1 sp of **new Motif**, ch 3, sk next dc and next ch-1 sp, sc in next dc, ch 3, sk next ch-1 sp and next dc, sc in next ch-1 sp, ch 3, sc in next ch-3 sp, ch 3, sc in next ch-1 sp, ch 3, sk next dc and next ch-1 sp, sc in next dc, ch 3, sk next ch-1 sp and next dc, (hdc, ch 5, hdc) in next ch-1 sp, ch 3, sk next dc and next ch-1 sp, sc in next dc, ch 3, sk next ch-1 sp and next dc, sc in next ch-1 sp, ch 3, join with sl st in beg sc. Fasten off.

LAST MOTIF2 (make 1 per tier)
Rnds 1-4:
Work same as Rnds 1-4 of First Motif1.

Rnd 5:
Placing Last Motif2 to the left of previous Motif made, ch 1, sc in last sp made, ch 3, sc in next ch-1 sp, ch 3, sk next dc and next ch-1 sp, sc in next dc, ch 3, sk next ch-1 sp and next dc, * hdc in next ch-1 sp, ch 2, sl st in third ch of corresponding ch-5 sp of **previous Motif**, ch 2, hdc in same ch-1 sp of **new Motif**, ch 1, sl st in second ch of next ch-3 sp of **previous Motif**, ch 1, sk next dc and next ch-1 sp of **new Motif**, sc in next dc, ch 1, sl st in second ch of next ch-3 sp of **previous Motif**, ch 1, sk next ch-1 sp and next dc of **new Motif**, sc in next ch-1 sp, ch 1, sl st in second ch of next ch-3 sp of **previous Motif**, ch 1, sc in next ch-3 sp of **new Motif**, ch 1, sl st in second ch of next ch-3 sp of **previous Motif**, ch 1, sc in next ch-1 sp of **new Motif**, ch 1, sl st in second ch of next ch-3 sp of **previous Motif**, ch 1, sk next dc and next ch-1 sp of **new Motif**, sc in next dc, ch 1, sl st in second ch of next ch-3 sp of **previous Motif**, ch 1, sk next ch-1 sp and next dc of **new Motif**, rep from * 2 times **more**, hdc in next ch-1 sp, ch 2, sl st in third ch of ch-5 sp of **previous Motif**, ch 2, hdc in same ch-1 sp of **new Motif**, ch 3, sk next dc and next ch-1 sp, sc in next dc, ch 3, sk next ch-1 sp and next dc, sc in next ch-1 sp, ch 3, join with sl st in beg sc. Fasten off.

Complete 3 more tiers of Motifs until there is a total of 5 Motif tiers.

SKIRT YOKE
Row 1:
With **wrong** side of Motifs facing, join thread with sc in any corner joining *(see Joining with Sc, page 95)*, *† (ch 2, sc in next ch-3 sp) 6 times, ch 2 †, sc in next corner joining, rep from * {15-16}{17-18-19} times **more**, then rep from † to † once, join with sl st in beg sc.

Row 2:
Ch 1, 2 sc in each ch-2 sp across: {238-252}{266-280-294} sc.

NOTE: Skirt opening is on the left side.

Row 3:
Ch 1, turn; sc in each sc across. Mark row for Buttonhole Border.

Row 4 (right side):
Ch 3 (**counts as first dc, now and throughout**), turn; dc in next {1-2}{0-1-2} sc *(see Zeros, page 95)*, 3 dc in next sc, (sk next 2 sc, sc in next sc, sk next 2 sc, 5 dc in next sc) {38-40}{43-45-47} times, sk next 2 sc, sc in next sc, sk next 2 sc, 3 dc in next sc, dc in last {1-2}{0-1-2} sc.

NOTE: Loop a short piece of thread around any stitch to mark Row 4 as **right** side.

Row 5:
Ch 1, turn; sc in first {2-3}{1-2-3} dc, * ch 2, 5dctog over next 5 sts, ch 2, sc in next st, rep from * {38-40}{43-45-47} times **more**, sc in last {2-3}{1-2-3} dc.

Row 6:
Ch 1, turn; sc in first {3-4}{2-3-4} sc, * 2 sc in next ch-2 sp, sc in next 5dctog, 2 sc in next ch-2 sp, sc in next sc, rep from * {38-40}{43-45-47} times **more**, sc in last {1-2}{0-1-2} sc: {238-252}{266-280-294} sc.

Row 7 (dec row):
Ch 1, turn; sc in first {8-4}{5-7-8} sc, 2sctog over next 2 sts, * sc in next {18-20}{21-22-23} sc, 2sctog over next 2 sc, rep from *10 times **more**, sc in last {8-4}{6-7-9} sts.

Row 8:
Ch 3, turn; dc in next {1-2}{0-1-2} sc, 3 dc in next sc, (sk next 2 sc, sc in next sc, sk next 2 sc, 5 dc in next sc) {36-38}{41-43-45} times **more**, sk next 2 sc, sc in next sc, sk next 2 sc, 3 dc in next sc, dc in last {1-2} {0-1-2} sc.

Row 9:
Ch 1, turn; sc in first {2-3}{1-2-3} dc, * ch 2, 5dctog over next 5 sts, ch 2, sc in next dc, rep from * {36-38} {41-43-45} times **more**, sc in last {2-3}{1-2-3} dc.

Row 10:
Ch 1, turn; sc in first {3-4}{2-3-4} sc, * 2 sc in next ch-2 sp, sc in next 5dctog, 2 sc in next ch-2 sp, sc in next sc, rep from * {36-38}{41-43-45} times **more**, sc in last {1-2}{0-1-2} sc: {226-240}{254-268-282} sc.

Row 11 (dec row):
Ch 1, turn; sc in first {4-3}{5-6-8} sc, 2sctog over next 2 sts, * sc in next {16-19}{20-21-22} sc, 2sctog over next 2 sc, rep from * {11-10} {10-10-10} times **more**, sc in last {4-4} {5-7-8} sc.

Row 12:
Ch 3, turn; dc in next {0-2}{0-1-2} sc, 3 dc in next sc, (sk next 2 sc, sc in next sc, sk next 2 sc, 5 dc in next sc) {34-36}{39-41-43} times **more**, sk next 2 sc, sc in next sc, sk next 2 sc, 3 dc in next sc, dc in last {1-2} {0-1-2} sc.

Row 13:
Ch 1, turn; sc in first {2-3}{1-2-3} dc, * ch 2, 5dctog over next 5 sts, ch 2, sc in next dc, rep from * {34-36} {39-41-43} times **more**, sc in last {1-3}{1-2-3} dc.

Row 14:
Ch 1, turn; sc in first {2-4}{2-3-4} sc, * 2 sc in next ch-2 sp, sc in next 5dctog, 2 sc in next ch-2 sp, sc in next sc, rep from * {34-36}{39-41-43} times **more**, sc in last {1-2}{0-1-2} dc: {213-228}{242-256-270} sc.

Row 15 (dec row):
Ch 1, turn; sc in first {3-5}{4-6-7} sc, 2sctog over next 2 sc, * sc in next {15-16}{19-20-21} sc, 2sctog over next 2 sc, rep from * {11-11} {10-10-10} times **more**, sc in last {4-5}{5-6-8} sc.

Row 16:
Ch 3, turn; dc in next {0-1}{0-1-2} sc, 3 dc in next sc, (sk next 2 sc, sc in next sc, sk next 2 sc, 5 dc in next sc) {32-34}{37-39-41} times **more**, sk next 2 sc, sc in next sc, sk next 2 sc, 3 dc in next sc, dc in last {0-2}{0-1-2} sc.

Row 17:
Ch 1, turn; sc in first {1-3}{1-2-3} dc, * ch 2, 5dctog over next 5 sts, ch 2, sc in next dc, rep from * {32-34} {37-39-41} times **more**, sc in last {1-2}{1-2-3} dc.

Row 18:
Ch 1, turn; sc in first {2-3}{2-3-4} sc, * 2 sc in next ch-2 sp, sc in next 5dctog, 2 sc in next ch-2 sp, sc in next sc, rep from * {32-34}{37-39-41} times **more**, sc in last {0-2}{0-1-2} sc: {200-215}{230-244-258} sc.

Row 19 (dec row):
Ch 1, turn; sc in first {3-4}{6-7-8} sc, 2sctog over next 2 sc, * sc in next {14-15}{16-17-18} sc, 2sctog over next 2 sc, rep from * 11 times **more**, sc in last {3-5}{6-7-8} sc.

Row 20:
Ch 3, turn; dc in next {2-1}{2-0-1} sc, 3 dc in next sc, (sk next 2 sc, sc in next sc, sk next 2 sc, 5 dc in next sc) {29-32}{34-37-39} times **more**, sk next 2 sc, sc in next sc, sk next 2 sc, 3 dc in next sc, dc in last {3-1} {3-1-2} sc.

Row 21:
Ch 1, turn; sc in first {4-2}{4-2-3} dc, * ch 2, 5dctog over next 5 sts, ch 2, sc in next dc, rep from * {29-32}{34-37-39} times **more**, sc in last {3-2}{3-1-2} dc.

Row 22:
Ch 1, turn; sc in first {4-3}{4-2-3} sc, * 2 sc in next ch-2 sp, sc in next 5dctog, 2 sc in next ch-2 sp, sc in next sc, rep from * {29-32}{34-37-39} times **more**, sc in last {3-1}{3-1-2} dc: {187-202}{217-231-245} sc.

Row 23 (dec row):
Ch 1, turn; sc in first {2-4}{5-6-7} sc, 2sctog over next 2 sc, * sc in next {13-14}{15-16-17} sc, 2sctog over next 2 sc, rep from * 11 times **more**, sc in last {3-4}{6-7-8} sc.

Row 24:
Ch 3, turn; dc in next {2-0}{2-0-1} sc, 3 dc in next st, (sk next 2 sc, sc in next st, sk next 2 sc, 5 dc in next st) {27-30}{32-35-37} times **more**, sk next 2 sc, sc in next sc, sk next 2 sc, 3 dc in next sc, dc in last {2-1} {2-0-1} sc.

Row 25:
Ch 1, turn; sc in first {3-2}{3-1-2} dc, * ch 2, 5dctog over next 5 sts, ch 2, sc in next dc, rep from * {27-30} {32-35-37} times **more**, sc in last {3-1}{3-1-2} dc.

Row 26:
Ch 1, turn; sc in first {4-2}{4-2-3} sc, * 2 sc in next ch-2 sp, sc in next 5dctog, 2 sc in next ch-2 sp, sc in next sc, rep from * {27-30}{32-35-37} times **more**, sc in last {2-1}{2-0-1} sc: {174-189}{204-218-232} sc.

Row 27 (dec row):
Ch 1, turn; sc in first {2-2}{5-6-7} sc, 2sctog over next 2 sc, * sc in next {12-12}{14-15-16} sc, 2sctog over next 2 sc, rep from * {11-12} {11-11-11} times **more**, sc in last {2-3}{5-6-7} sc.

Row 28:
Ch 3, turn; dc in next {1-2}{1-2-0} sc, 3 dc in next st, (sk next 2 sc, sc in next sc, sk next 2 sc, 5 dc in next sc) {25-27}{30-32-35} times **more**, sk next 2 sc, sc in next sc, sk next 2 sc, 3 dc in next sc, dc in last {2-3} {2-3-1} sc.

Row 29:
Ch 1, turn; sc in first {3-4}{3-4-2} dc, * ch 2, 5dctog over next 5 sts, ch 2, sc in next dc, rep from * {25-27} {30-32-35} times **more**, sc in last {2-3}{2-3-1} dc.

Row 30:
Ch 1, turn; sc in first {3-4}{3-4-2} sc, * 2 sc in next ch-2 sp, sc in next 5dctog, 2 sc in next ch-2 sp, sc in next sc, rep from * {25-27}{30-32-35} times **more**, sc in last {2-3}{2-3-1} sc: {161-175}{191-205-219} sc.
Fasten off.

BUTTONHOLE BORDER
Row 1:
With **right** side facing and working along side of left edge, join thread with sc around sc at end of marked row, 2 sc around dc at end of next row, (sc around sc at end of next 3 rows, 2 sc around dc at end of next row) 6 times, sc around st at end of next row; working along top edge, 3 sc in first sc, sc in next {159-173}{189-203-217} sc, 3 sc in last sc; working along side of right edge, sc around sc at end of next row, 2 sc around dc at end of next row, (sc

around sc at end of next 3 rows, 2 sc around dc at end of next row) 6 times, sc around sc at end of marked row: {233-247}{263-277-291} sc.

Row 2 (Buttonhole Row):
Ch 1, turn; sc in first 35 sc, 3 sc in next sc, sc in next {161-175} {191-205-219} sc, 3 sc in next sc, (ch 2, sk next 2 sc, sc in next 6 sc) 4 times, ch 2, sk next 2 sc, sc in last sc.

Row 3:
Ch 1, turn; sc in first sc, ch 2, sc in center of sc just made, sk next ch, sc in next ch, * (ch 2, sc in center of sc just made, sk next sc, sc in next sc) 3 times, ch 2, sc in center of sc just made, sk next ch, sc in next ch, rep from * 3 times **more**, ch 2, sc in center of sc just made, sk next sc, sc in next sc, ch 2, sc in center of sc just made, sc in same corner sc, (ch 2, sc in center of last sc made, sk next sc, sc in next sc) {82-89}{97-104-111} times, ch 2, sc in center of last sc made, sc in same corner sc, (ch 2, sc in center of sc just made, sk next sc, sc in next sc) 18 times. Fasten off.

Sew buttons to right side to correspond with buttonholes on left side.

BOTTOM BORDER
Rnd 1:
With **right** side facing and working along bottom edge, join with sc in any joining between Motifs, *† (ch 3, sc in next ch-3 sp) 3 times, (dc, ch 2, dc) in next sc, sc in next ch-3 sp, (ch 3, sc in next ch-3 sp) twice †, ch 3, sc in joining between Motifs, rep from * {15-16}{17-18-19} times **more**, then rep from † to † once, join with dc in beg sc to form last sp.

Rnd 2:
Ch 1, sc in last sp made, (dc, ch 2, dc) in same sc as joining-dc, sc in next ch-3 sp, *† (ch 3, sc in next ch-3 sp) twice, ch 1, 5 dc in next ch-2 sp, ch 1, sc in next ch-3 sp †, (ch 3, sc in next ch-3 sp) twice, (dc, ch 2, dc) in next sc, sc in next ch-3 sp, rep from * {15-16}{17-18-19} times **more**, then rep from † to † once, ch 3, sc in next ch-3 sp, join with dc in beg sc to form last sp.

Rnd 3:
Ch 1, sc in last sp made, ch 1, 5 dc in next ch-2 sp, ch 1, sc in next ch-3 sp, *† ch 3, sc in next ch-3 sp, ch 1, dc in next dc, [ch 1, (dc, ch 1, dc) in next dc, ch 1, dc in next dc] twice, ch 1, sc in next ch-3 sp †, ch 3, sc in next ch-3 sp, ch 1, 5 dc in next ch-2 sp, ch 1, sc in next ch-3 sp, rep from * {15-16}{17-18-19} times **more**, then rep from † to † once, join with dc in beg sc to form last sp.

Rnd 4:
Ch 1, sc in last sp made, *† ch 1, dc in next dc, [ch 1, (dc, ch 1, dc) in next dc, ch 1, dc in next dc] twice, ch 1, sc in next ch-3 sp, ch 1, dc in next dc, [ch 1, (dc, ch 1, dc) in next dc, ch 1, dc in next dc] 3 times †, ch 1, sc in next ch-3 sp, rep from * {15-16}{17-18-19} times **more**, then rep from † to † once, join with sc in beg sc to form last sp.

Rnd 5:
Ch 1, pull up a loop in last sp made and in next ch-1 sp, YO, pull through all loops on hook, *† (ch 3, sc in next sp) 6 times, ch 3, (pull up a loop in next sp) twice, YO, pull through all loops on hook, (ch 3, sc in next sp) 9 times, ch 3 †, (pull up a loop in next sp) twice, YO, pull through all loops on hook, rep from * {15-16}{17-18-19} times **more**, then rep from † to † once, join with sl st in beg sc. Fasten off.

Yesterday once more

Women of the 1940s were lucky—they wore fashions with interesting details like these almost every day. But if you can crochet, you can also slip into this nostalgic outfit whenever you like. The peplum jacket has a drawstring waist, inset pleats, and rounded lapels. It looks perfect with shorts or trousers. The stripe-and-dot skirt has some fascinating features of its own—the points marching around the hem are created to be self-pleating.

top

FINISHED CHEST SIZE:

X-Small:	32^1/$_2$" (82.5 cm)	Large:	43^1/$_4$" (110 cm)
Small:	36" (91.5 cm)	X-Large:	46^3/$_4$" (119 cm)
Medium:	39^1/$_2$" (100.5 cm)		

Instructions are written with sizes X-Small and Small in the first set of braces { } and with sizes Medium, Large, and X-Large in the second set of braces. Instructions will be easier to read if you circle all the numbers pertaining to your size. If only one number is given, it applies to all sizes.

MATERIALS

Bedspread Weight Cotton Thread (size 10) [350 yards (320 meters) per ball]: {4-4}{5-5-6} balls
Steel crochet hook, size 7 (1.65 mm)
  or size needed for gauge
^{1}/$_2$" (13 mm) Buttons: 8
Sewing needle and matching thread

GAUGE:

Working in pattern:
  4 shells (2 dc, ch 2, 2 dc + dc) = 3^1/$_2$" (9 cm)
  8 rows = 3" (7.5 cm)

SPECIAL STITCHES:

FPdc: YO, insert hook from **front** to **back** around post of specified st *(Fig. 2, page 95)*, YO, pull up a loop, (YO, pull through 2 loops on hook) twice.

BPdc: YO, insert hook from **back** to **front** around post of specified st *(Fig. 2, page 95)*, YO, pull up a loop, (YO, pull through 2 loops on hook) twice.

Hdc in top of dc just made: YO, insert hook through one horizontal bar and one vertical bar of specified stitch *(Fig. 5, page 95)*, YO, pull up a loop, YO, pull through all loops on hook.

BODY

Top is worked in one piece to armholes.

Drawstring Row:
Ch {219-243}{267-291-315}, sc in second ch from hook, ch 1, sk next ch, sc in next ch, (ch 2, sk next 2 chs, sc in next ch) {71-79}{87-95-103} times, ch 1, sk next ch, sc in last ch.

Row 1 (right side):
Ch 3 (**counts as first dc, now and throughout**), turn; sk next ch-1 sp, (2 dc, ch 2, 2 dc) in next ch-2 sp, * dc in next ch-2 sp, (2 dc, ch 2, 2 dc) in next ch-2 sp, rep from * {34-38} {42-46-50} times **more**, sk last ch-1 sp, dc in last sc: {36-40} {44-48-52} ch-2 sps.

NOTE: Loop a short piece of thread around any stitch to mark Row 1 as **right** *side.*

Rows 2 thru {18-18}{20-20-20}:
Ch 3, turn; * sk next 2 dc, (2 dc, ch 2, 2 dc) in next ch-2 sp, sk next 2 dc, dc in next dc, rep from * across.

ARMHOLE SHAPING

Ch 3, turn, [sk next 2 dc, (2 dc, ch 2, 2 dc) in next ch-2 sp, sk next 2 dc, dc in next dc] {9-9}{10-10-11} times, [sk next 2 dc, (dc, hdc, ch 1, hdc, dc) in next ch-2 sp, sk next 2 dc, dc in next dc] {0-2}{2-4-4} times *(see Zeros, page 95)*, [sk next 2 dc, (2 dc, ch 2, 2 dc) in next ch-2 sp, sk next 2 dc, dc in next dc] {18-18}{20-20-22} times, [sk next 2 dc, (dc, hdc, ch 1, hdc, dc) in next ch-2 sp, sk next 2 dc, dc in next dc] {0-2}{2-4-4} times, [sk next 2 dc, (2 dc, ch 2, 2 dc) in next ch-2 sp, sk next 2 dc, dc in next dc] {9-9}{10-10-11} times.

LEFT FRONT

Row 1:
Ch 3, turn; [sk next 2 dc, (2 dc, ch 2, 2 dc) in next ch-2 sp, sk next 2 dc, dc in next dc] {8-8}{9-9-10} times, sk next 2 dc, 2 dc in next ch-2 sp, leave rem sts unworked.

Row 2:
Ch 2, turn; sk next dc, dc in next dc, [sk next 2 dc, (2 dc, ch 2, 2 dc) in next ch-2 sp, sk next 2 dc, dc in next dc] {8-8}{9-9-10} times.

Row 3:
Ch 3, turn; [sk next 2 dc, (2 dc, ch 2, 2 dc) in next ch-2 sp, sk next 2 dc, dc in next dc] {8-8}{9-9-10} times, leave ch-2 unworked.

Row 4:
Ch 3, turn; [sk next 2 dc, (2 dc, ch 2, 2 dc) in next ch-2 sp, sk next 2 dc, dc in next dc] {7-7}{8-8-9} times, sk next 2 dc, (2 dc, ch 2, dc, hdc) in next ch-2 sp, sk next 2 dc, sc in last dc.

Row 5:
Turn; sl st in first 2 sts, ch 1, skip next dc, (sc, ch 2, 2 dc) in next ch-2 sp, sk next 2 dc, dc in next dc, [sk next 2 dc, (2 dc, ch 2, 2 dc) in next ch-2 sp, sk next 2 dc, dc in next dc] {7-7}{8-8-9} times.

Row 6:
Ch 3, turn; [sk next 2 dc, (2 dc, ch 2, 2 dc) in next ch-2 sp, sk next 2 dc, dc in next dc] {7-7}{8-8-9} times, sk next 2 dc, dc in next ch-2 sp, leave rem sc unworked.

Row 7:
Ch 2, turn; dc in next dc, [sk next 2 dc, (2 dc, ch 2, 2 dc) in next ch-2 sp, sk next 2 dc, dc in next dc] {7-7}{8-8-9} times.

Row 8:
Ch 3, turn; [sk next 2 dc, (2 dc, ch 2, 2 dc) in next ch-2 sp, sk next 2 dc, dc in next dc] {6-6}{7-7-8} times, sk next 2 dc, (2 dc, ch 2, dc, hdc) in next ch-2 sp, sk next 2 dc, sc in last dc, leave ch-2 unworked.

Row 9:
Turn; sl st in first 2 sts, ch 1, skip next dc, (sc, ch 2, 2 dc) in next ch-2 sp, sk next 2 dc, dc in next dc, [sk next 2 dc, (2 dc, ch 2, 2 dc) in next ch-2 sp, sk next 2 dc, dc in next dc] {6-6}{7-7-8} times.

Row 10:
Ch 3, turn; [sk next 2 dc, (2 dc, ch 2, 2 dc) in next ch-2 sp, sk next 2 dc, dc in next dc] {6-6}{7-7-8} times, sk next 2 dc, dc in next ch-2 sp, leave rem sc unworked.

Row 11:
Ch 2, turn; dc in next dc, [sk next 2 dc, (2 dc, ch 2, 2 dc) in next ch-2 sp, sk next 2 dc, dc in next dc] {6-6}{7-7-8} times.

Row 12:
Ch 3, turn; [sk next 2 dc, (2 dc, ch 2, 2 dc) in next ch-2 sp, sk next 2 dc, dc in next dc] {5-5}{6-6-7} times, sk next 2 dc, (2 dc, ch 2, dc, hdc) in next ch-2 sp, sk next 2 dc, sc in last dc, leave ch-2 unworked.

Row 13:
Turn; sl st in first 2 sts, ch 1, skip next dc, (sc, ch 2, 2 dc) in next ch-2 sp, sk next 2 dc, dc in next dc, [sk next 2 dc, (2 dc, ch 2, 2 dc) in next ch-2 sp, sk next 2 dc, dc in next dc] {5-5}{6-6-7} times.

Row 14:
Ch 3, turn; [sk next 2 dc, (2 dc, ch 2, 2 dc) in next ch-2 sp, sk next 2 dc, dc in next dc] {5-5}{6-6-7} times, sk next 2 dc, dc in next ch-2 sp, leave rem sc unworked.

Row 15:
Ch 2, turn; dc in next dc, [sk next 2 dc, (2 dc, ch 2, 2 dc) in next ch-2 sp, sk 2 dc, dc in next dc] {5-5}{6-6-7} times, do **not** fasten off.

Medium, Large, and X-Large Only:
Row 16:
Ch 3, turn; [sk next 2 dc, (2 dc, ch 2, 2 dc) in next ch-2 sp, sk next 2 dc, dc in next dc] {5}{5-6} times, sk next 2 dc, (2 dc, ch 2, dc, hdc) in next ch-2 sp, sk next 2 dc, sc in last dc, leave ch-2 unworked.

Row 17:
Turn; sl st in first 2 sts, ch 1, (sc, ch 2, 2 dc) in next ch-2 sp, sk next 2 dc, dc in next dc, [sk next 2 dc, (2 dc, ch 2, 2 dc) in next ch-2 sp, sk next 2 dc, dc in next dc] {5}{5-6} times.

Row 18:
Ch 3, turn; [sk next 2 dc, (2 dc, ch 2, 2 dc) in next ch-2 sp, sk next 2 dc, dc in next dc] {5}{5-6} times, sk next 2 dc, dc in next ch-2 sp, leave rem sc unworked.

Row 19:
Ch 2, turn; dc in next dc, [sk next 2 dc, (2 dc, ch 2, 2 dc) in next ch-2 sp, sk next 2 dc, dc in next dc] {5}{5-6} times, do **not** fasten off.

LEFT SHOULDER

X-Small and Small Only:
Rows 1-5:
Ch 3, turn; [sk next 2 dc, (2 dc, ch 2, 2 dc) in next ch-2 sp, sk next 2 dc, dc in next dc] 5 times.

Medium Only:
Row 1:
Ch 3, turn; [sk next 2 dc, (2 dc, ch 2, 2 dc) in next ch-2 sp, sk next 2 dc, dc in next dc] 5 times, leave ch-2 unworked.

Large and X-Large Only:
Rows 1-3:
Ch 3, turn; [sk next 2 dc, (2 dc, ch 2, 2 dc) in next ch-2 sp, sk next 2 dc, dc in next dc] {5-6} times.

LEFT SHOULDER SHAPING

Row 1:
Ch 3, turn; [sk next 2 dc, (2 dc, ch 2, 2 dc) in next ch-2 sp, sk next 2 dc, dc in next dc] {2-2}{2-2-3} times, mark last dc made, [sk next 2 dc, (dc, hdc, ch 1, hdc, dc) in next ch-2 sp, sk next 2 dc, hdc in next dc] twice, ch 2, sc in next ch-2 sp, ch 2, sc in last dc. Fasten off.

Row 2:
Join thread with sc in marked dc *(see Joining with Sc, page 95)*, ch 2, sc in next ch-2 sp, ch 2, sk next 2 dc, hdc in next dc, [sk next 2 dc, (dc, hdc, ch 1, hdc, dc) in next ch-2 sp, sk next 2 dc, dc in next dc] {1-1}{1-1-2} time(s). Fasten off.

BACK

Row 1:
With **wrong** side facing, join thread with slip st in next unworked ch-2 sp of Body, ch 3, dc in same sp, sk next 2 dc, dc in next dc, [sk next 2 dc, (2 dc, ch 2, 2 dc) in next ch-2 sp, sk next 2 dc, dc in next dc] {16-16} {18-18-20} times, sk next 2 dc, 2 dc in next ch-2 sp, leave rem sts unworked.

Row 2:
Ch 2, turn; sk next dc, dc in next dc, [sk next 2 dc, (2 dc, ch 2, 2 dc) in next ch-2 sp, sk next 2 dc, dc in next dc] {15-15}{17-17-19} times, sk next 2 dc, (2 dc, ch 2, 2 dc) in next ch-2 sp, sk next 2 dc, (YO, pull up a loop in next st, YO, pull through 2 loops on hook) twice, YO, pull through all loops on hook.

Rows 3 thru {20-20}{20-22-22}:
Ch 3, turn; [sk next 2 dc, (2 dc, ch 2, 2 dc) in next ch-2 sp, sk next 2 dc, dc in next dc] {16-16}{18-18-20} times.

LEFT SHOULDER

Row 1:
Ch 1, turn; sc in first st, ch 2, sk next 2 dc, sc in next ch-2 sp, ch 2, sk next 2 dc, hdc in next dc, [sk next 2 dc, (dc, hdc, ch 1, hdc, dc) in next ch-2 sp, sk next 2 dc, dc in next dc] twice, [sk next 2 dc, (2 dc, ch 2, 2 dc) in next ch-2 sp, sk next 2 dc, dc in next dc] {2-2}{2-2-3} times, sk next 2 dc, 2 dc in next ch-2 sp.

Row 2:
Ch 2, turn; sk next dc, dc in next dc, [(dc, hdc, ch 1, hdc, dc) in next ch-2 sp, sk next 2 dc, hdc in next dc] {1-1}{1-1-2} time(s), ch 2, sk next 2 dc, sc in next ch-2 sp, ch 2, sk next 2 dc, sc in next dc. Fasten off.

RIGHT SHOULDER
Row 1:
With **wrong** side facing, sk next {4-4}{6-6-6} unworked ch-2 sps of Back and join thread with sl st in next ch-2 sp, ch 3, dc in same sp, sk next 2 dc, dc in next dc, [sk next 2 dc, (2 dc, ch 2, 2 dc) in next ch-2 sp, sk next 2 dc, dc in next dc] {1-1}{1-1-2} time(s), sk next 2 dc, (2 dc, ch 2, 2 dc) in next ch-2 sp, sk next

2 dc, hdc in next dc, mark hdc just made, [sk next 2 dc, (dc, hdc, ch 1, hdc, dc) in next ch-2 sp, sk next 2 dc, hdc in next dc] twice, ch 2, sk next 2 dc, sc in next ch-2 sp, ch 2, sk next 2 dc, sc in last dc. Fasten off.

Row 2:
With **right** side facing, join thread with sc in marked hdc, ch 2, sk next 2 dc, sc in next ch-2 sp, sk next 2 dc, hdc in next dc, [sk next 2 dc, (dc, hdc, ch 1, hdc, dc) in next ch-2 sp, sk next 2 dc, dc in next dc] {0-0}{0-0-1} time(s), sk next 2 dc, (dc, hdc, ch 1, hdc, dc) in next ch-2 sp, sk next 2 dc, YO, pull up a loop in next dc, YO, pull through 2 loops on hook, sk next dc, YO, pull up a loop in last dc, YO, pull through 2 loops on hook, YO, pull through all loops on hook. Fasten off.

RIGHT FRONT

Row 1:
With **wrong** side facing, join thread with sl st in next unworked ch-2 sp of Body, ch 3, dc in same sp, sk next 2 dc, dc in next dc, [sk next 2 dc, (2 dc, ch 2, 2 dc) in next ch-2 sp, sk next 2 dc, dc in next dc] {8-8} {9-9-10} times.

Row 2:
Ch 3, turn; [sk next 2 dc, (2 dc, ch 2, 2 dc) in next ch-2 sp, sk next 2 dc, dc in next dc] {7-7}{8-8-9} times, sk next 2 dc, (2 dc, ch 2, 2 dc) in next ch-2 sp, sk next 2 dc, YO, pull up a loop in next dc, YO, pull through 2 loops on hook, sk next dc, YO, pull up a loop in last dc, YO, pull through 2 loops on hook, YO, pull through all loops on hook.

Row 3:
Ch 3, turn; [sk next 2 dc, (2 dc, ch 2, 2 dc) in next ch-2 sp, sk next 2 dc, dc in next dc] {8-8}{9-9-10} times.

Row 4:
Ch 1, turn; sc in first st, sk next 2 dc, (hdc, dc, ch 2, 2 dc) in next ch-2 sp, sk next 2 dc, dc in next dc, [sk next 2 dc, (2 dc, ch 2, 2 dc) in next ch-2 sp, sk next 2 dc, dc in next dc] {7-7}{8-8-9} times.

Row 5:
Ch 3, turn; [sk next 2 dc, (2 dc, ch 2, 2 dc) in next ch-2 sp, sk next 2 dc, dc in next dc] {7-7}{8-8-9} times, dc in next ch-2 sp, YO, pull up a loop in same ch-2 sp, YO, pull through 2 loops on hook, YO, pull up a loop in next dc, YO, pull through 2 loops on hook, YO, pull through all loops on hook.

Row 6:
Ch 3, turn; sk next dc, dc in next dc, [sk next 2 dc, (2 dc, ch 2, 2 dc) in next ch-2 sp, sk next 2 dc, dc in next dc] {7-7}{8-8-9} times.

Row 7:
Ch 3, turn; [sk next 2 dc, (2 dc, ch 2, 2 dc) in next ch-2 sp, sk next 2 dc, dc in next dc] {6-6}{7-7-8} times, sk next 2 dc, (2 dc, ch 2, 2 dc) in next ch-2 sp, sk next 2 dc, YO, pull up a loop in next dc, YO, pull through 2 loops on hook, YO, pull up a loop in last dc, YO, pull through 2 loops on hook, YO, pull through all loops on hook.

Row 8:
Ch 1, turn; sc in first st, sk next 2 dc, (hdc, dc, ch 2, 2 dc) in next ch-2 sp, sk next 2 dc, dc in next dc, [sk next 2 dc, (2 dc, ch 2, 2 dc) in next ch-2 sp, sk next 2 dc, dc in next dc] {6-6}{7-7-8} times.

Row 9:
Ch 3, turn; [sk next 2 dc, (2 dc, ch 2, 2 dc) in next ch-2 sp, sk next 2 dc, dc in next dc] {6-6}{7-7-8} times, dc in next ch-2 sp, YO, pull up a loop in same ch-2 sp, YO, pull through 2 loops on hook, YO, pull up a loop in next dc, YO, pull through 2 loops on hook, YO, pull through all loops on hook.

Row 10:
Ch 3, turn; sk next dc, dc in next dc, [sk next 2 dc, (2 dc, ch 2, 2 dc) in next ch-2 sp, sk next 2 dc, dc in next dc] {6-6}{7-7-8} times.

Row 11:
Ch 3, turn; [sk next 2 dc, (2 dc, ch 2, 2 dc) in next ch-2 sp, sk next 2 dc, dc in next dc] {5-5}{6-6-7} times, sk next 2 dc, (2 dc, ch 2, 2 dc) in next ch-2 sp, sk next 2 dc, YO, pull up a loop in next dc, YO, pull through 2 loops on hook, YO, pull up a loop in last dc, YO, pull through 2 loops on hook, YO, pull through all loops on hook.

Row 12:
Ch 1, turn; sc in first st, sk next 2 dc, (hdc, dc, ch 2, 2 dc) in next ch-2 sp, sk next 2 dc, dc in next dc, [sk next 2 dc, (2 dc, ch 2, 2 dc) in next ch-2 sp, sk next 2 dc, dc in next dc] {5-5}{6-6-7} times.

Row 13:
Ch 3, turn; [sk next 2 dc, (2 dc, ch 2, 2 dc) in next ch-2 sp, sk next 2 dc, dc in next dc] {5-5}{6-6-7} times, dc in next ch-2 sp, YO, pull up a loop in same ch-2 sp, YO, pull through 2 loops on hook, YO, pull up a loop in next dc, YO, pull through 2 loops on hook, YO, pull through all loops on hook.

Row 14:
Ch 3, turn; sk next dc, dc in next dc, [sk next 2 dc, (2 dc, ch 2, 2 dc) in next ch-2 sp, sk next 2 dc, dc in next dc] {5-5}{6-6-7} times.

Row 15:
Ch 3, turn; sk next 2 dc, (2 dc, ch 2, 2 dc) in next ch-2 sp, sk next 2 dc, dc in next dc] {4-4}{5-5-6} times, sk next 2 dc, (2 dc, ch 2, 2 dc) in next ch-2 sp, sk next 2 dc, YO, pull up a loop in next dc, YO, pull through 2 loops on hook, YO, pull up a loop in last dc, YO, pull through 2 loops on hook, YO, pull through all loops on hook.

X-Small and Small Only:
Skip to Right Shoulder.

Row 16:

Ch 1, turn; sc in first st, sk next 2 dc, (hdc, dc, ch 2, 2 dc) in next ch-2 sp, sk next 2 dc, dc in next dc, [sk next 2 dc, (2 dc, ch 2, 2 dc) in next ch-2 sp, sk next 2 dc, dc in next dc] {5-5-6} times.

Row 17:

Ch 3, turn; [sk next 2 dc, (2 dc, ch 2, 2 dc) in next ch-2 sp, sk next 2 dc, dc in next dc] {5-5-6} times, dc in next ch-2 sp, YO, pull up a loop in same ch-2 sp, YO, pull through 2 loops on hook, YO, pull up a loop in next dc, YO, pull through 2 loops on hook, YO, pull through all loops on hook.

Row 18:

Ch 3, turn; sk next dc, dc in next dc, [sk next 2 dc, (2 dc, ch 2, 2 dc) in next ch-2 sp, sk next 2 dc, dc in next dc] {5-5-6} times.

Row 19:

Ch 3, turn; [sk next 2 dc, (2 dc, ch 2, 2 dc) in next ch-2 sp, sk next 2 dc, dc in next dc] {4-4-5} times, sk next 2 dc, (2 dc, ch 2, 2 dc) in next ch-2 sp, sk next 2 dc, (YO, pull up a loop in next dc, YO, pull through 2 loops on hook) twice, YO, pull through all loops on hook.

RIGHT SHOULDER

X-Small and Small Only:
Rows 1-5:

Ch 3, turn; [sk next 2 dc, (2 dc, ch 2, 2 dc) in next ch-2 sp, sk next 2 dc, dc in next dc] 5 times.

Medium Only:
Row 1:

Ch 3, turn; [sk next 2 dc, (2 dc, ch 2, 2 dc) in next ch-2 sp, sk next 2 dc, dc in next dc] 5 times.

Large and X-Large Only:
Rows 1-3:

Ch 3, turn; [sk next 2 dc, (2 dc, ch 2, 2 dc) in next ch-2 sp, sk next 2 dc, dc in next dc] {5-6} times.

RIGHT SHOULDER SHAPING
Row 1:

Ch 1, turn; sc in first st, ch 2, sk next 2 dc, sc in next ch-2 sp, ch 2, [sk next 2 dc, hdc in next st, sk next 2 dc, (dc, hdc, ch 1, hdc, dc) in next ch-2 sp] twice, [sk next 2 dc, dc in next st, sk next 2 dc, (2 dc, ch 2, 2 dc) in next ch-2 sp] {2-2}{2-2-3} times, sk next 2 dc, dc in last dc.

Row 2:

Ch 3, turn; [sk next 2 dc, (dc, hdc, ch 1, hdc, dc) in next ch-2 sp, sk next 2 dc, dc in next dc] {0-0}{0-0-1} times, sk next 2 dc, (dc, hdc, ch 1, hdc, dc) in next ch-2 sp, sk next 2 dc, hdc in next dc, ch 2, sk next 2 dc, sc in next ch-2 sp, ch 2, sk next 2 dc, sc in last dc. Fasten off.

Sew shoulder seams.

BOTTOM PLEATED BORDER
Row 1:

With **right** side facing and working in sps and free loops of beginning ch *(Fig. 3b, page 95)*, join thread with sl st in ch at base of first sc, ch 3, sk next ch-1 sp, [(2 dc, ch 2, 2 dc) in next ch-2 sp, dc in next ch-2 sp] {3-4}{4-5-5} times, † (2 dc, ch 2, 2 dc) in next ch-2 sp, (dc, ch 1, 5 dc, ch 2, 5 dc, ch 1, dc) in next ch-2 sp †, [(2 dc, ch 2, 2 dc) in next ch-2 sp, dc in next ch-2 sp] {8-9}{10-11-12} times, rep from † to † once, [(2 dc, ch 2, 2 dc) in next ch-2 sp, dc in next ch-2 sp] {4-4}{5-5-6} times, rep from † to † once, [(2 dc, ch 2, 2 dc) in next

ch-2 sp, dc in next ch-2 sp] {4-4}
{5-5-6} times, rep from † to † once,
[(2 dc, ch 2, 2 dc) in next ch-2 sp,
dc in next ch-2 sp] {8-9}{10-11-12}
times, rep from † to † once, [(2 dc,
ch 2, 2 dc) in next ch-2 sp, dc in next
ch-2 sp] {3-4}{4-5-5} times, (2 dc,
ch 2, 2 dc) in next ch-2 sp, sk next
ch-1 sp, dc in ch at base of last sc.

Row 2:
Ch 3, turn; [sk next 2 dc, (2 dc, ch 2,
2 dc) in next ch-2 sp, sk next 2 dc,
dc in next dc] {3-4}{4-5-5} times,
† sk next 2 dc, (2 dc, ch 2, 2 dc)
in next ch-2 sp, sk next 2 dc, BPdc
around next dc, ch 1, 2 dc in next
ch-1 sp, dc in next dc, sk next dc,
FPdc around next dc, sk next dc,
dc in next dc, (2 dc, ch 2, 2 dc)
in next ch-2 sp, dc in next dc, sk
next dc, FPdc around next dc, sk
next dc, dc in next dc, 2 dc in next
ch-1 sp, ch 1, BPdc around next dc †,
[sk next 2 dc, (2 dc, ch 2, 2 dc) in
next ch-2 sp, sk next 2 dc, dc in next
dc] {8-9}{10-11-12} times, rep from
† to † once, [sk next 2 dc, (2 dc, ch 2,
2 dc) in next ch-2 sp, sk next 2 dc,
dc in next dc] {4-4}{5-5-6} times,
rep from † to † once, [sk next 2 dc,
(2 dc, ch 2, 2 dc) in next ch-2 sp, sk
next 2 dc, dc in next dc] {4-4}{5-5-6}
times, rep from † to † once, [sk next
2 dc, (2 dc, ch 2, 2 dc) in next
ch-2 sp, sk next 2 dc, dc in next dc]
{8-9}{10-11-12} times, rep from
† to † once, [sk next 2 dc, (2 dc, ch 2,
2 dc) in next ch-2 sp, sk next 2 dc, dc
in next dc] {4-5}{5-6-6} times.

Row 3:
Ch 3, turn; [sk next 2 dc, (2 dc,
ch 2, 2 dc) in next ch-2 sp, sk next
2 dc, dc in next dc] {3-4}{4-5-5}
times, † sk next 2 dc, (2 dc, ch 2,
2 dc) in next ch-2 sp, sk next 2 dc,
FPdc around next dc, ch 1, 2 dc in
next ch-1 sp, dc in next 2 dc, sk next
dc, BPdc around next dc, sk next dc,

dc in next 2 dc, (2 dc, ch 2, 2 dc)
in next ch-2 sp, dc in next 2 dc, sk
next dc, BPdc around next dc, sk
next dc, dc in next 2 dc, 2 dc in next
ch-1 sp, ch 1, FPdc around next dc †,
[sk next 2 dc, (2 dc, ch 2, 2 dc) in
next ch-2 sp, sk next 2 dc, dc in next
dc] {8-9}{10-11-12} times, rep from
† to † once, [sk next 2 dc, (2 dc, ch 2,
2 dc) in next ch-2 sp, sk next 2 dc,
dc in next dc] {4-4}{5-5-6} times,
rep from † to † once, [sk next 2 dc,
(2 dc, ch 2, 2 dc) in next ch-2 sp, sk
next 2 dc, dc in next dc] {4-4}{5-5-6}
times, rep from † to † once, [sk next
2 dc, (2 dc, ch 2, 2 dc) in next
ch-2 sp, sk next 2 dc, dc in next dc]
{8-9} {10-11-12} times, rep from
† to † once, [sk next 2 dc, (2 dc, ch 2,
2 dc) in next ch-2 sp, sk next 2 dc, dc
in next dc] {4-5}{5-6-6} times.

Row 4:
Ch 3, turn; [sk next 2 dc, (2 dc, ch 2,
2 dc) in next ch-2 sp, sk next 2 dc, dc
in next dc] {3-4}{4-5-5} times, † sk
next 2 dc, (2 dc, ch 2, 2 dc) in next
ch-2 sp, sk next 2 dc, BPdc around
next dc, ch 1, 2 dc in next ch-1 sp, dc
in next 3 dc, sk next dc, FPdc around
next dc, sk next dc, dc in next 3 dc,
(2 dc, ch 2, 2 dc) in next ch-2 sp,
dc in next 3 dc, sk next dc, FPdc
around next dc, sk next dc, dc in
next 3 dc, 2 dc in next ch-1 sp, ch 1,
BPdc around next dc †, [sk next 2
dc, (2 dc, ch 2, 2 dc) in next ch-2 sp,
sk next 2 dc, dc in next dc] {8-9}
{10-11-12} times, rep from † to †
once, [sk next 2 dc, (2 dc, ch 2, 2 dc)
in next ch-2 sp, sk next 2 dc, dc in
next dc] {4-4}{5-5-6} times, rep from

† to † once, [sk next 2 dc, (2 dc, ch 2, 2 dc) in next ch-2 sp, sk next 2 dc, dc in next dc] {4-4}{5-5-6} times, rep from † to † once, [sk next 2 dc, (2 dc, ch 2, 2 dc) in next ch-2 sp, sk next 2 dc, dc in next dc] {8-9} {10-11-12} times, rep from † to † once, [sk next 2 sc, (2 dc, ch 2, 2 dc) in next ch-2 sp, sk next 2 dc, dc in next dc] {4-5}{5-6-6} times.

Row 5:

Ch 3, turn; [sk next 2 dc, (2 dc, ch 2, 2 dc) in next ch-2 sp, sk next 2 dc, dc in next dc] {3-4}{4-5-5} times, † sk next 2 dc, (2 dc, ch 2, 2 dc) in next ch-2 sp, sk next 2 dc, FPdc around next dc, ch 1, 2 dc in next ch-1 sp, dc in next 4 dc, sk next dc, BPdc around next dc, sk next dc, dc in next 4 dc, (2 dc, ch 2, 2 dc) in next ch-2 sp, dc in next 4 dc, sk next dc, BPdc around next dc, sk next dc, dc in next 4 dc, 2 dc in next ch-1 sp, ch 1, FPdc around next dc †, [sk next 2 dc, (2 dc, ch 2, 2 dc) in next ch-2 sp, sk next 2 dc, dc in next dc] {8-9}{10-11-12} times, rep from † to † once, [sk next 2 dc, (2 dc, ch 2, 2 dc) in next ch-2 sp, sk next 2 dc, dc in next dc] {4-4} {5-5-6} times, rep from † to † once, [sk next 2 dc, (2 dc, ch 2, 2 dc) in next ch-2 sp, sk next 2 dc, dc in next dc] {4-4} {5-5-6} times, rep from † to † once, [sk next 2 dc, (2 dc, ch 2, 2 dc) in next ch-2 sp, sk next 2 dc, dc in next dc] {8-9}{10-11-12} times, rep from † to † once, [sk next 2 dc, (2 dc, ch 2, 2 dc) in next ch-2 sp, sk next 2 dc, dc in next dc] {4-5}{5-6-6} times.

Row 6:

Ch 3, turn; [sk next 2 dc, (2 dc, ch 2, 2 dc) in next ch-2 sp, sk next 2 dc, dc in next dc] {3-4}{4-5-5} times, † sk next 2 dc, (2 dc, ch 2, 2 dc) in next ch-2 sp, sk next 2 dc, BPdc around next dc, ch 1, 2 dc in next ch-1 sp, dc in next 5 dc, sk next dc, FPdc around next dc, sk next dc, dc in next 5 dc, (2 dc, ch 2, 2 dc) in next ch-2 sp, dc in next 5 dc, sk next dc, FPdc around next dc, sk next dc, dc in next 5 dc, 2 dc in next ch-1 sp, ch 1, BPdc around next dc †, [sk next 2 dc, (2 dc, ch 2, 2 dc) in next ch-2 sp, sk next 2 dc, dc in next dc] {8-9}{10-11-12} times, rep from † to † once, [sk next 2 dc, (2 dc, ch 2, 2 dc) in next ch-2 sp, sk next 2 dc, dc in next dc] {4-4}{5-5-6} times, rep from † to † once, [sk next 2 dc, (2 dc, ch 2, 2 dc) in next ch-2 sp, sk next 2 dc, dc in next dc] {4-4}{5-5-6} times, rep from † to † once, [sk next 2 dc, (2 dc, ch 2, 2 dc) in next ch-2 sp, sk next 2 dc, dc in next dc] {8-9}{10-11-12} times, rep from † to † once, [sk next 2 dc, (2 dc, ch 2, 2 dc) in next ch-2 sp, sk next 2 dc, dc in next dc] {4-5}{5-6-6} times.

Row 7:

Ch 3, turn; [sk next 2 dc, (2 dc, ch 2, 2 dc) in next ch-2 sp, sk next 2 dc, dc in next dc] {3-4}{4-5-5} times, † sk next 2 dc, (2 dc, ch 2, 2 dc) in next ch-2 sp, sk next 2 dc, FPdc around next dc, ch 1, 2 dc in next ch-1 sp, dc in next 6 dc, sk next dc, BPdc around next dc, sk next dc, dc in next 6 dc, (2 dc, ch 2, 2 dc) in next ch-2 sp, dc in next 6 dc, sk next dc, BPdc around next dc, sk next dc, dc in next 6 dc, 2 dc in next ch-1 sp, ch 1, FPdc around next dc †, [sk next 2 dc, (2 dc, ch 2, 2 dc) in next ch-2 sp, sk next 2 dc, dc in next dc] {8-9}{10-11-12} times, rep from † to † once, [sk next 2 dc, (2 dc, ch 2, 2 dc) in next ch-2 sp, sk next 2 dc, dc in next dc] {4-4}{5-5-6} times, rep from † to † once, [sk next 2 dc, (2 dc, ch 2, 2 dc) in next ch-2 sp, sk next 2 dc, dc in next dc] {4-4}{5-5-6} times, rep from † to † once, [sk next 2 dc, (2 dc, ch 2, 2 dc) in next ch-2 sp, sk next 2 dc, dc in next dc] {8-9}{10-11-12} times, rep from † to † once, [sk next 2 dc, (2 dc, ch 2, 2 dc) in next ch-2 sp, sk next 2 dc, dc in next dc] {4-5}{5-6-6} times.

Row 8:

Ch 3, turn; [sk next 2 dc, (2 dc, ch 2, 2 dc) in next ch-2 sp, sk next 2 dc, dc in next dc] {3-4}{4-5-5} times, † sk next 2 dc, (2 dc, ch 2, 2 dc) in next ch-2 sp, sk next 2 dc, BPdc around next dc, ch 1, 2 dc in ch-1 sp, dc in next 7 dc, sk next dc, FPdc around next dc, sk next dc, dc in next 7 dc, (2 dc, ch 2, 2 dc) in next ch-2 sp, dc in next 7 dc, sk next dc, FPdc around next dc, sk next dc, dc in next 7 dc, 2 dc in next ch-1 sp, ch 1, BPdc around next dc †, [sk next 2 dc, (2 dc, ch 2, 2 dc) in next ch-2 sp, sk next 2 dc, dc in next dc] {8-9} {10-11-12} times, rep from † to † once, [sk next 2 dc, (2 dc, ch 2, 2 dc) in next ch-2 sp, sk next 2 dc, dc in next dc] {4-4} {5-5-6} times, rep from † to † once, [sk next 2 dc, (2 dc, ch 2, 2 dc) in next ch-2 sp, sk next 2 dc, dc in next dc] {4-4} {5-5-6} times, rep from † to † once, [sk next 2 dc, (2 dc, ch 2, 2 dc) in next ch-2 sp, sk next 2 dc, dc in next dc] {8-9}{10-11-12} times, rep from † to † once, [sk next 2 dc, (2 dc, ch 2, 2 dc) in next ch-2 sp, sk next 2 dc, dc in next dc] {4-5}{5-6-6} times.

Row 9:

X-Small, Small, and Medium Only:

Ch 3, turn; [sk next 2 dc, (2 dc, ch 2, hdc in top of last dc made, 2 dc) in next ch-2 sp, sk next 2 dc, dc in next dc] {3-4}{4} times, † sk next 2 dc, (2 dc, ch 2, hdc in top of last dc made, 2 dc) in next ch-2 sp, sk next 2 dc, FPdc around next dc, ch 1, 2 dc in next ch-1 sp, dc in next 8 dc, sk next dc, BPdc around next dc, sk next dc, dc in next 8 dc, (2 dc, ch 2, hdc in top of last dc made, 2 dc) in next ch-2 p, dc in next 8 dc, sk next dc, BPdc around next dc, sk next dc, dc in next 8 dc, 2 dc in next ch-1 sp, ch 1, FPdc around next dc †, [sk next 2 dc, (2 dc, ch 2, hdc in top of last dc made, 2 dc) in next ch-2 sp, sk next 2 dc, dc in next dc] {8-9}{10} times, rep from † to † once, [sk next 2 dc, (2 dc, ch 2, hdc in top of last dc made, 2 dc) in next ch-2 sp, sk next 2 dc, dc in next dc] {4-5}{5} times, rep from † to † once, [sk next 2 dc, (2 dc, ch 2, hdc in top of last dc made, 2 dc) in next ch-2 sp, sk next 2 dc, dc in next dc] {4-4}{5} times, rep from † to † once, [sk next 2 dc, (2 dc, ch 2, hdc in top of last dc made, 2 dc) in next ch-2 sp, sk next 2 dc, dc in next dc] {8-9}{10} times, rep from † to † once, [sk next 2 dc, (2 dc, ch 2, hdc in top of last dc made, 2 dc) in next ch-2 sp, sk next 2 dc, dc in next dc] {4-5}{5} times. Fasten off.

Row 9:

Large and X-Large Only:

Ch 3, turn; [sk next 2 dc, (2 dc, ch 2, 2 dc) in next ch-2 sp, sk next 2 dc, dc in next dc] 5 times, † sk next 2 dc, (2 dc, ch 2, 2 dc) in next ch-2 sp, sk next 2 dc, FPdc around next dc, ch 1, 2 dc in next ch-1 sp, dc in next 8 dc, sk next dc, BPdc around next dc, sk next dc, dc in next 8 dc, (2 dc, ch 2, 2 dc) in next ch-2 sp, dc in next 8 dc, sk next dc, BPdc around next dc, sk next dc, dc in next 8 dc, 2 dc in next ch-1 sp, ch 1, FPdc around next dc †, [sk next 2 dc, (2 dc, ch 2, 2 dc) in next ch-2 sp, sk next 2 dc, dc in next dc] {11-12} times, rep from † to † once, [sk next 2 dc, (2 dc, ch 2, 2 dc) in next ch-2 sp, sk next 2 dc, dc in next dc] {5-6} times, rep from † to † once, [sk next 2 dc, (2 dc, ch 2, 2 dc) in next ch-2 sp, sk next 2 dc, dc in next dc] {5-6} times, rep from † to † once, [sk next 2 dc, (2 dc, ch 2, 2 dc) in next ch-2 sp, sk next 2 dc, dc in next dc] {11-12} times, rep from † to † once, [sk next 2 dc, (2 dc, ch 2, 2 dc) in next ch-2 sp, sk next 2 dc, dc in next dc] 6 times.

Row 10:

Large and X-Large Only:

Ch 3, turn; [sk next 2 dc, (2 dc, ch 2, 2 dc) in next ch-2 sp, sk next 2 dc, dc in next dc] 5 times, † sk next 2 dc, (2 dc, ch 2, 2 dc) in next ch-2 sp, sk next 2 dc, BPdc around next dc, ch 1, 2 dc in next ch-1 sp, dc in next 9 dc, sk next dc, FPdc around next dc, sk next dc, dc in next 9 dc, (2 dc, ch 2, 2 dc) in next ch-2 sp, dc in next 9 dc, sk next dc, FPdc around next dc, sk next dc, dc in next 9 dc, 2 dc in next ch-1 sp, ch 1, BPdc around next dc †, [sk next 2 dc, (2 dc, ch 2, 2 dc) in next ch-2 sp, sk next 2 dc, dc in next dc] {11-12} times, rep from † to † once, [sk next 2 dc, (2 dc, ch 2, 2 dc) in next ch-2 sp, sk next 2 dc, dc in next dc] {5-6} times, rep from † to † once, [sk next 2 dc, (2 dc, ch 2, 2 dc) in next ch-2 sp, sk next 2 dc, dc in next dc] {5-6} times, rep from † to † once, [sk next 2 dc, (2 dc, ch 2, 2 dc) in next ch-2 sp, sk next 2 dc, dc in next dc] {11-12} times, rep from † to † once, [sk next 2 dc, (2 dc, ch 2, 2 dc) in next ch-2 sp, sk next 2 dc, dc in next dc] 6 times.

Row 11:

Large and X-Large Only:

Ch 3, turn; [sk next 2 dc, (2 dc, ch 2, hdc in top of last dc made, 2 dc) in next ch-2 sp, sk next 2 dc, dc in next dc] 5 times, † sk next 2 dc, (2 dc, ch 2, hdc in top of last dc made, 2 dc) in next ch-2 sp, sk next 2 dc, FPdc around next dc, ch 1, 2 dc in next ch-1 sp, dc in next 10 dc, sk next dc, BPdc around next dc, sk next dc, dc in next 10 dc, (2 dc, ch 2, hdc in top of last dc made, 2 dc) in next ch-2 sp, dc in next 10 dc, sk next dc, BPdc around next dc, sk next dc, dc in next 10 dc, 2 dc in next ch-1 sp, ch 1, FPdc around next dc †, [sk next 2 dc, (2 dc, ch 2, hdc in top of last dc made, 2 dc) in next ch-2 sp, sk next 2 dc, dc in next dc] {11-12} times, rep from † to † once, [sk next 2 dc, (2 dc, ch 2, hdc in top of last dc made, 2 dc) in next ch-2 sp, sk next 2 dc, dc in next dc] {5-6} times, rep from † to † once, [sk next 2 dc, (2 dc, ch 2, hdc in top of last dc made, 2 dc) in next ch-2 sp, sk next 2 dc, dc in next dc] {5-6} times, rep from † to † once, [sk next 2 dc, (2 dc, ch 2, hdc in top of last dc made, 2 dc) in next ch-2 sp, sk next 2 dc, dc in next] {11-12} times, rep from † to † once, [sk next 2 dc, (2 dc, ch 2, hdc in top of last dc made, 2 dc) in next ch-2 sp, sk next 2 dc, dc in next dc] 6 times.
Fasten off.

WAIST DRAWSTRING

Ch 3, dc in third ch from hook, * ch 2, dc in top of dc just made, rep from * until drawstring measures 12" (30.5 cm) longer than waist measurement. Fasten off. Trim ends.

Weave drawstring in and out of ch-2 sps of Drawstring Row, skipping one ch-2 sp at back.

SLEEVE (make 2)
Drawstring Row:
Ch {87-99}{99-123-123}, sc in second ch from hook, ch 1, sk next ch, sc in next ch, (ch 2, sk next 2 chs, sc in next ch) across to last 2 chs, ch 1, sk next ch, sc in last ch.

Row 1 (right side):
Ch 3, turn; sk first ch-1 sp, (2 dc, ch 2, 2 dc) in next ch-2 sp, * dc in next ch-2 sp, (2 dc, ch 2, 2 dc) in next ch-2 sp, rep from * across to last ch-1 sp, sk next ch-1 sp, dc in last sc.

NOTE: Mark Row 1 as **right** side.

Row 1a:
Large and X-Large Only:
Ch 3, turn; [sk next 2 dc, (2 dc, ch 2, 2 dc) in next ch-2 sp, sk next 2 dc, dc in next dc] 20 times.

Row 2:
Ch 3, turn; [sk next 2 dc, (dc, hdc, ch 1, hdc, dc) in next ch-2 sp, sk next 2 dc, dc in next dc] {0-1}{1-2-2} time(s), [sk next 2 dc, (2 dc, ch 2, 2 dc) in next ch-2 sp, sk next 2 dc, dc in next dc] {14-14}{14-16-16} times, [sk next 2 dc, (dc, hdc, ch 1, hdc, dc) in next ch-2 sp, sk next 2 dc, dc in next dc] {0-1}{1-2-2} time(s).

Row 3:
Turn; sl st across to first ch-2 sp, ch 3, dc in same sp, sk next 2 dc, dc in next dc, [sk next 2 dc, (2 dc, ch 2, 2 dc) in next ch-2 sp, sk next 2 dc, dc in next dc] {12-12}{12-14-14} times, sk next 2 dc, 2 dc in next ch-2 sp, leave rem 3 sts unworked.

Row 4:
Ch 2, turn; sk next dc, dc in next dc, [sk next 2 dc, (2 dc, ch 2, 2 dc) in next ch-2 sp, sk next 2 dc, dc in next dc] {11-11}{11-13-13} times, sk next 2 dc, (2 dc, ch 2, 2 dc) in next ch-2 sp, sk next 2 dc, YO, pull up a loop in next dc, YO, pull through 2 loops on hook, sk next dc, YO, pull up a loop in last dc, YO, pull through 2 loops on hook, YO, pull through all loops on hook.

Row 5:
Ch 1, turn; sc in first st, sk next 2 dc, (hdc, dc, ch 2, 2 dc) in next ch-2 sp, sk next 2 dc, dc in next dc, [sk next 2 dc, (2 dc, ch 2, 2 dc) in next ch-2 sp, sk next 2 dc, dc in next dc] {10-10} {10-12-12} times, sk next 2 dc, (2 dc, ch 2, dc, hdc) in next ch-2 sp, sk next 2 dc, sc in last dc, leave rem ch-2 unworked.

Row 6:
Turn; sl st in first 2 sts, ch 1, (sc, ch 2, 2 dc) in next ch-2 sp, sk next 2 dc, dc in next dc, [sk next 2 dc, (2 dc, ch 2, 2 dc) in next ch-2 sp, sk next 2 dc, dc in next dc] {10-10}{10-12-12} times, dc in next ch-2 sp, YO, pull up a loop in same ch-2 sp, YO, pull through 2 loops on hook, YO, pull up a loop in next dc, YO, pull through 2 loops on hook, YO, pull through all loops on hook, leave rem 2 sts unworked.

Row 7:
Ch 3, turn; sk first st, dc in next dc, [sk next 2 dc, (2 dc, ch 2, 2 dc) in next ch-2 sp, sk next 2 dc, dc in next dc] {10-10}{10-12-12} times, sk next 2 dc, dc in next ch-2 sp, leave rem sc unworked.

Row 8:
Ch 2, turn; dc in next dc, [sk next 2 dc, (2 dc, ch 2, 2 dc) in next ch-2 sp, sk next 2 dc, dc in next dc] {9-9} {9-11-11} times, sk next 2 dc, (2 dc, ch 2, 2 dc) in next ch-2 sp, sk next 2 dc, YO, pull up a loop in next dc, YO, pull through 2 loops on hook, sk next st, YO, pull up a loop in last dc, YO, pull through 2 loops on hook, YO, pull through all loops on hook.

Row 9:
Ch 1, turn; sc in first st, sk next 2 dc, (hdc, dc, ch 2, 2 dc) in next ch-2 sp, sk next 2 dc, dc in next dc, [sk next 2 dc, (2 dc, ch 2, 2 dc) in next ch-2 sp, sk next 2 dc, dc in next dc] {8-8}{8-10-10} times, sk next 2 dc, (2 dc, ch 2, dc, hdc) in next ch-2 sp, sk next 2 dc, sc in last dc, leave ch-2 unworked.

Row 10:
Turn; sl st in first 2 sts, ch 1, (sc, ch 2, 2 dc) in next ch-2 sp, sk next 2 dc, dc in next dc, [sk next 2 dc, (2 dc, ch 2, 2 dc) in next ch-2 sp, sk next 2 dc, dc in next dc] {8-8}{8-10-10} times, dc in next ch-2 sp, YO, pull up a loop in same ch-2 sp, YO, pull through 2 loops on hook, YO, pull up a loop in next dc, YO, pull through 2 loops on hook, YO, pull through all loops on hook, leave remaining 2 sts unworked.

Row 11:
Ch 3, turn; sk first st, dc in next dc, [sk next 2 dc, (2 dc, ch 2, 2 dc) in next ch-2 sp, sk next 2 dc, dc in next dc] {8-8}{8-10-10} times, sk next 2 dc, dc in next ch-2 sp, leave rem sc unworked.

Row 12:
Ch 2, turn; dc in next dc, [sk next 2 dc, (2 dc, ch 2, 2 dc) in next ch-2 sp, sk next 2 dc, dc in next dc] {7-7} {7-9-9} times, sk next 2 dc, (2 dc, ch 2, 2 dc) in next ch-2 sp, sk next 2 dc, YO, pull up a loop in next dc, YO, pull through 2 loops on hook, sk next dc, YO, pull up a loop in last dc, YO, pull through 2 loops on hook, YO, pull through all loops on hook.

Row 13:
Ch 1, turn; sc in first st, sk next 2 dc, (2 sc, ch 2, 2 dc) in next ch-2 sp, sk next 2 dc, dc in next dc, [sk next 2 dc, (2 dc, ch 2, 2 dc) in next ch-2 sp, sk next 2 dc, dc in next dc] {6-6}{6-8-8} times, sk next 2 dc, (2 dc, ch 2, 2 sc) in next ch-2 sp, sk next 2 dc, sc in last dc, leave ch-2 unworked.

Row 14:
Turn; sl st in first 2 sts, ch 1, skip next sc, sc in next ch-2 sp, ch 3, sk next 2 dc, dc in next dc, [sk next 2 dc, (2 dc, ch 2, 2 dc) in next ch-2 sp, sk next 2 dc, dc in next dc] {6-6}{6-8-8} times, sk next 2 dc, dc in next ch-2 sp, leave rem 3 sc unworked.

Row 15:
Ch 1, turn; skip first st, sc in next dc, sk next 2 dc, (2 sc, ch 2, 2 dc) in next ch-2 sp, sk next 2 dc, dc in next dc,

[sk next 2 dc, (2 dc, ch 2, 2 dc) in next ch-2 sp, sk next 2 dc, dc in next dc] {4-4} {4-6-6} times, sk next 2 sc, (2 dc, ch 2, 2 sc) in next ch-2 sp, sk next 2 dc, sc in last dc.

Row 16:
Turn; sl st in first 2 sts, ch 1, skip next sc, sc in next ch-2 sp, ch 3, sk next 2 dc, dc in next dc, [sk next 2 dc, (2 dc, ch 2, 2 dc) in next ch-2 sp, sk next 2 dc, dc in next dc] {4-4} {4-6-6} times, sk next 2 dc, dc in next ch-2 sp, leave rem 3 sc unworked.

Row 17:
X-Small, Small, and Medium Only:
Ch 1, turn; skip first st, sc in next dc, sk next 2 dc, (2 sc, 2 hdc) in next ch-2 sp, sk next 2 dc, dc in next dc, [sk next 2 dc, (dc, hdc, ch 1, hdc, dc) in next ch-2 sp, sk next 2 dc, dc in

next dc] twice, sk next 2 dc, (2 hdc, 2 sc) in next ch-2 sp, sk next 2 dc, sc in next dc, leave rem dc unworked. Fasten off.

Large and X-Large Only:
Ch 1, turn; sc in next dc, sk next 2 dc, (2 sc, 2 hdc) in next ch-2 sp, sk next 2 dc, dc in next dc, [sk next 2 dc, (2 dc, ch 2, 2 dc) in next ch-2 sp, sk next 2 dc, dc in next dc] 4 times, sk next 2 dc, (2 hdc, 2 sc) in next ch-2 sp, sk next 2 dc, sc in next dc, leave rem dc unworked.

Row 18:
Large and X-Large Only:
Turn; sl st in first 4 sts, ch 1, skip next hdc, sc in next dc, sk next 2 dc, (2 sc, 2 hdc) in next ch-2 sp, sk next 2 dc, dc in next dc, [sk next 2 dc, (dc, hdc,

ch 1, hdc, dc) in next ch-2 sp, sk next 2 dc, dc in next dc] twice, sk next 2 dc, (2 hdc, 2 sc) in next ch-2 sp, sk next 2 dc, sc in next dc, leave rem 5 sts unworked. Fasten off.

SLEEVE PLEATED BORDER
Row 1:
With **right** side facing and working in sps and free loops of beginning ch, join thread with sl st in ch at base of first sc, ch 3, sk next ch-1 sp, [(2 dc, ch 2, 2 dc) in next ch-2 sp, dc in next ch-2 sp] {6-7}{7-9-9} times, (2 dc, ch 2, 2 dc) in next ch-2 sp, (dc, ch 1, 5 dc, ch 2, 5 dc, ch 1, dc) in next ch-2 sp, [(2 dc, ch 2, 2 dc) in next ch-2 sp, dc in next ch-2 sp] {6-7} {7-9-9} times, (2 dc, ch 2, 2 dc) in next ch-2 sp, sk next ch-1 sp, dc in ch at base of last sc.

Row 2:

Ch 3, turn; [sk next 2 dc, (2 dc, ch 2, 2 dc) in next ch-2 sp, sk next 2 dc, dc in next dc] {6-7}{7-9-9} times, sk next 2 dc, (2 dc, ch 2, 2 dc) in next ch-2 sp, sk next 2 dc, BPdc around next dc, ch 1, 2 dc in next ch-1 sp, dc in next dc, sk next dc, FPdc around next dc, sk next dc, dc in next dc, (2 dc, ch 2, 2 dc) in next ch-2 sp, dc in next dc, sk next dc, FPdc around next dc, sk next dc, dc in next dc, 2 dc in next ch-1 sp, ch 1, BPdc around next dc, [sk next 2 dc, (2 dc, ch 2, 2 dc) in next ch-2 sp, sk next 2 dc, dc in next dc] {7-8}{8-10-10} times.

Row 3:

Ch 3, turn; [sk next 2 dc, (2 dc, ch 2, 2 dc) in next ch-2 sp, sk next 2 dc, dc in next dc] {6-7}{7-9-9} times, sk next 2 dc, (2 dc, ch 2, 2 dc) in next ch-2 sp, sk next 2 dc, FPdc around next dc, ch 1, 2 dc in next ch-1 sp, dc in next 2 dc, sk next dc, BPdc around next dc, sk next dc, dc in next 2 dc, (2 dc, ch 2, 2 dc) in next ch-2 sp, dc in next 2 dc, sk next dc, BPdc around next dc, sk next dc, dc in next 2 dc, 2 dc in next ch-1 sp, ch 1, FPdc around next dc, [sk next 2 dc, (2 dc, ch 2, 2 dc) in next ch-2 sp, sk next 2 dc, dc in next dc] {7-8}{8-10-10} times.

Row 4:

Ch 3, turn; [sk next 2 dc, (2 dc, ch 2, 2 dc) in next ch-2 sp, sk next 2 dc, dc in next dc] {6-7}{7-9-9} times, sk next 2 dc, (2 dc, ch 2, 2 dc) in next ch-2 sp, sk next 2 dc, BPdc around next dc, ch 1, 2 dc in next ch-1 sp, dc in next 3 dc, sk next dc, FPdc around next dc, sk next dc, dc in next 3 dc, (2 dc, ch 2, 2 dc) in next ch-2 sp, dc in next 3 dc, sk next dc, FPdc around next dc, sk next dc, dc in next 3 dc, 2 dc in next ch-1 sp, ch 1, BPdc around next dc, [sk next 2 dc, (2 dc, ch 2, 2 dc) in next ch-2 sp, sk next 2 dc, dc in next dc] {7-8}{8-10-10} times.

Row 5:

Ch 3, turn; [sk next 2 dc, (2 dc, ch 2, 2 dc) in next ch-2 sp, sk next 2 dc, dc in next dc] {6-7}{7-9-9} times, sk next 2 dc, (2 dc, ch 2, 2 dc) in next ch-2 sp, sk next 2 dc, FPdc around next dc, ch 1, 2 dc in next ch-1 sp, dc in next 4 dc, sk next dc, BPdc around next dc, sk next dc, dc in next 4 dc, (2 dc, ch 2, 2 dc) in next ch-2 sp, dc in next 4 dc, sk next dc, BPdc around next dc, sk next dc, dc in next 4 dc, 2 dc in next ch-1 sp, ch 1, FPdc around next dc, [sk next 2 dc, (2 dc, ch 2, 2 dc) in next ch-2 sp, sk next 2 dc, dc in next dc] {7-8}{8-10-10} times.

Row 6:

Ch 3, turn; [sk next 2 dc, (2 dc, ch 2, 2 dc) in next ch-2 sp, sk next 2 dc, dc in next dc] {6-7}{7-9-9} times, sk next 2 dc, (2 dc, ch 2, 2 dc) in next ch-2 sp, sk next 2 dc, BPdc around next dc, ch 1, 2 dc in next ch-1 sp, dc in next 5 dc, sk next dc, FPdc around next dc, sk next dc, dc in next 5 dc, (2 dc, ch 2, 2 dc) in next ch-2 sp, dc in next 5 dc, sk next dc, FPdc around next dc, sk next dc, dc in next 5 dc, 2 dc in next ch-1 sp, ch 1, BPdc around next dc, [sk next 2 dc, (2 dc, ch 2, 2 dc) in next ch-2 sp, sk next 2 dc, dc in next dc] {7-8}{8-10-10} times.

Row 7:

Ch 3, turn; [sk next 2 dc, (2 dc, ch 2, hdc in top of last dc made, 2 dc) in next ch-2 sp, sk next 2 dc, dc in next dc] {6-7}{7-9-9} times, sk next 2 dc, (2 dc, ch 2, hdc in top of last dc made, 2 dc) in next ch-2 sp, sk next 2 dc, FPdc around next dc, ch 1, 2 dc in next ch-1 sp, dc in next 6 dc, sk next dc, BPdc around next dc, sk next dc, dc in next 6 dc, (2 dc, ch 2, hdc in top of last dc made, 2 dc) in next ch-2 sp, dc in next 6 dc, sk next dc, BPdc around next dc, sk next dc, dc in next 6 dc, 2 dc in next ch-1 sp, ch 1, FPdc around next dc, [sk next 2 dc, (2 dc, ch 2, hdc in top of last dc made, 2 dc) in next ch-2 sp, sk next 2 dc, dc in next dc] {7-8}{8-10-10} times. Fasten off.

Sew sleeve seams. Inset sleeves into sleeve openings.

SLEEVE DRAWSTRING (make 2)
Ch 3, dc in third ch from hook, * ch 2, dc in top of dc just made, rep from * until drawstring measures 10" (25.5 cm) longer than Sleeve Drawstring Row. Fasten off. Trim ends.

Weave drawstring in and out of ch-2 sps of Drawstring Row skipping ch-1 sps on sides of seam.

FRONT EDGING AND COLLAR

Row 1:
With **wrong** facing and working along side of Left Front, join thread with sc around dc at end of last row of Bottom Pleated Border, (2 hdc, ch 2, 2 dc) around dc at end of next row, dc around dc at end of next row, † (2 dc, ch 2, 2 dc) around dc at end of next row, dc around dc at end of next row †, rep from † to † 2 times **more**, sk Drawstring Row, rep from † to † {11-11}{12-12-12} times, mark last (2 dc, ch 2, 2 dc) group made for placement of top button, (2 dc, ch 2, 2 dc) around sc at end of next row, sk next hdc, dc in next dc, [(2 dc, ch 2, 2 dc) in ch-2 sp at end of next row, dc around dc at end of next row, (2 dc, ch 2, 2 dc) around turning ch at end of next row, sk sc of next row, dc in next hdc]{2-2}{3-3-3} times, (2 dc, ch 2, 2 dc) in ch-2 sp at end of next row, dc around dc at end of next row, (2 dc, ch 2, 2 dc) around turning ch at end of next row, dc around dc at end of next row, rep from † to † {3-3}{1-2-2} times; working along back neck edge, (2 dc, ch 2, 2 dc)

around turning ch at end of next row, dc around dc at end of next row, [(2 dc, ch 2, 2 dc) in next ch-2 sp, sk next 2 dc, dc in next dc, sk next 2 dc] {5-5}{7-7-7} times, (2 dc, ch 2, 2 dc) in next ch-2 sp, dc around ch-3 at end of next row, (2 dc, ch 2, 2 dc) around dc at end of next row; working along Right Front edge, dc around dc at end of next row, rep from † to † {3-3} {1-2-2} time(s), [(2 dc, ch 2, 2 dc) around dc at end of next row, dc around turning ch at end of next row, (2 dc, ch 2, 2 dc) around dc at end of next row, dc around sc at end of next row], {2-2}{3-3-3} times, (2 dc, ch 2,

2 dc) around dc at end of next row, dc around turning ch at end of next row, (2 dc, ch 2, 2 dc) around dc at end of next row, sk next dc, dc in next hdc, (2 dc, ch 2, 2 dc) around sc at end of next row, dc around dc at end of next row, rep from † to † {10-10} {11-11-11} times, (2 dc, ch 2, 2 dc) around dc at end of next row, sk Drawstring Row, dc around dc at end of next row, rep from † to † 3 times, (2 dc, ch 2, 2 hdc) around dc at end of next row, sc around dc at end of last row: {58-58}{62-64-64} ch-2 sps.

85

Row 2:
Turn; skip first sc, sl st in next 2 hdc and in next ch-2 sp, sl st in next 2 dc, ch 1, sc in next dc, sk next 2 dc, (2 hdc, ch 2, hdc in top of last dc made, 2 dc) in next ch-2 sp, sk next 2 dc, dc in next dc, [sk next 2 dc, (2 dc, ch 2, hdc in top of last dc made, 2 dc) in next ch-2 sp, sk next 2 dc, dc in next dc] {13-13}{14-14-14} times, [sk next 2 dc, (2 dc, ch 2, 2 dc) in next ch-2 sp, sk next 2 dc, dc in next dc] {28-28}{30-32-32} times, mark last dc made, [sk next 2 dc, (2 dc, ch 2, hdc in top of last dc made, 2 dc) in next ch-2 sp, sk next 2 dc, dc in next dc] {13-13}{14-14-14} times, sk next 2 dc, (2 dc, ch 2, hdc in top of last dc made, 2 hdc) in next ch-2 sp, sk next 2 dc, sc in next dc, leave rem sts unworked. Fasten off.

Row 3:
With **wrong** side facing, join thread with sc in marked dc, sk next 2 dc, (2 hdc, ch 2, 2 dc) in next ch-2 sp, sk next 2 dc, dc in next dc, [sk next 2 dc, (2 dc, ch 2, 2 dc) in next ch-2 sp, sk next 2 dc, dc in next dc] {26-26}{28-30-30} times, sk next 2 dc, (2 dc, ch 2, 2 hdc) in next ch-2 sp, sk next 2 dc, sc in next dc.

Row 4:
Turn; skip first sc, sl st in next 2 hdc and in next ch-2 sp, sl st in next 2 dc, ch 1, sc in next dc, sk next 2 dc, (2 hdc, ch 2, 2 dc) in next ch-2 sp, sk next 2 dc, dc in next dc, [sk next 2 dc, (2 dc, ch 2, 2 dc) in next ch-2 sp, sk next 2 dc, dc in next dc] {24-24}{26-28-28} times, sk next 2 dc, (2 dc, ch 2, 2 hdc) in next ch-2 sp, sk next 2 dc, sc in next dc.

Row 5:
Turn; skip first sc, sl st in next 2 hdc, sl st in next ch-2 sp and in next 2 dc, ch 1, sc in next dc, sk next 2 dc, (2 hdc, ch 2, 2 dc) in next ch-2 sp, sk next 2 dc, dc in next dc, [sk next 2 dc, (2 dc, ch 2, 2 dc) in next ch-2 sp, sk next 2 dc, dc in next dc] {22-22}{24-26-26} times, sk next 2 dc, (2 dc, ch 2, 2 hdc) in next ch-2 sp, sk next 2 dc, sc in next dc.

Row 6:
Turn; skip first sc, sl st in next 2 hdc and in next ch-2 sp, sl st in next 2 dc, ch 1, sc in next dc, sk next 2 dc, (2 hdc, ch 2, 2 dc) in next ch-2 sp, sk next 2 dc, dc in next dc, [sk next 2 dc, (2 dc, ch 2, 2 dc) in next ch-2 sp, sk next 2 dc, dc in next dc] {20-20}{22-24-24} times, sk next 2 dc, (2 dc, ch 2, 2 hdc) in next ch-2 sp, sk next 2 dc, sc in next dc.

Row 7:

Turn; skip first sc, sl st in next 2 hdc, sl st in next ch-2 sp and in next 2 dc, ch 1, sc in next dc, sk next 2 dc, (2 hdc, ch 2, 2 dc) in next ch-2 sp, sk next 2 dc, dc in next dc, [sk next 2 dc, (2 dc, ch 2, 2 dc) in next ch-2 sp, sk next 2 dc, dc in next dc] {18-18} {20-22-22} times, sk next 2 dc, (2 dc, ch 2, 2 hdc) in next ch-2 sp, sk next 2 dc, sc in next dc.

Row 8:

Turn; skip first sc, sl st in next 2 hdc and in next ch-2 sp, sl st in next 2 dc, ch 1, sc in next dc, sk next 2 dc, (2 hdc, ch 2, 2 dc) in next ch-2 sp, sk next 2 dc, dc in next dc, [sk next 2 dc, (2 dc, ch 2, 2 dc) in next ch-2 sp, sk next 2 dc, dc in next dc] {16-16} {18-20-20} times, sk next 2 dc, (2 dc, ch 2, 2 hdc) in next ch-2 sp, sk next 2 dc, sc in next dc.

Row 9:

Turn; skip first sc, sl st in next 2 hdc, sl st in next ch-2 sp and in next 2 dc, ch 1, sc in next dc, sk next 2 dc, (2 hdc, ch 2, hdc in top of last dc made, 2 dc) in next ch-2 sp, sk next 2 dc, dc in next dc, [sk next 2 dc, (2 dc, ch 2, hdc in top of last dc made, 2 dc) in next ch-2 sp, sk next 2 dc, dc in next dc] {14-14} {16-18-18} times, sk next 2 dc, (2 dc, ch 2, hdc in top of last dc made, 2 hdc) in next ch-2 sp, sk next 2 dc, sc in next dc. Fasten off.

Working down left side, sew first button over marked dc-group on Row 1 of Collar. Sew second button over next dc-group, (sk next two dc-groups, sew buttons over next two dc-groups) 3 times.

skirt

◼◼◼◻ INTERMEDIATE

FINISHED HIP SIZE:

X-Small:	39" (99 cm)	Large:	48" (122 cm)
Small:	42" (106.5 cm)	X-Large:	51" (129.5 cm)
Medium:	45" (114.5 cm)		

Instructions are written with sizes X-Small and Small in the first set of braces { } and with sizes Medium, Large, and X-Large in the second set of braces. Instructions will be easier to read if you circle all the numbers pertaining to your size. If only one number is given, it applies to all sizes.

MATERIALS

Bedspread Weight Cotton Thread (size 10)
[350 yards (320 meters) per ball]:
Ecru - {4-5}{5-5-6} balls
Blue - 1 ball
Green - 1 ball
Steel crochet hook, size 7 (1.65 mm)
or size needed for gauge
Sewing needle and matching thread
Lightweight material for lining
Skirt pattern for lining (Butterick #3134 used for model)

GAUGE:

Motif measures 3" (7.5 cm) square.

SPECIAL STITCHES:

2dctog: (YO, insert hook in specified st or sp, YO, pull up a loop, YO, pull through 2 loops on hook) twice, YO, pull through all loops on hook.

3dctog: (YO, insert hook in specified st or sp, YO, pull up a loop, YO, pull through 2 loops on hook) 3 times, YO, pull through all loops on hook.

Sl st in center of sc just made: Insert hook through one horizontal bar and one vertical bar of specified st *(Fig. 5, page 95)*, YO, pull through all loops on hook.

Hdc in top of dc just made: YO, insert hook through one horizontal bar and one vertical bar of specified stitch *(Fig. 5, page 95)*, YO, pull up a loop, YO, pull through all loops on hook.

Dc in top of dc just made: YO, insert hook through one horizontal bar and one vertical bar of specified stitch *(Fig. 5, page 95)*, YO, pull up a loop, YO, pull through 2 loops on hook, YO, pull through rem loops on hook.

DRAWSTRING

With Ecru, ch 3, dc in third ch from hook, * ch 2, dc in top of dc just made, rep from * until drawstring measures {45-48}{51-54-57}"/ {114.5-122}{129.5-137-145} cm. Fasten off. Trim ends.

WAISTBAND

With Ecru, ch {234-252} {270-288-306}, join with sl st to form ring taking care not to twist ch.

Rnd 1:

Ch 4 (**counts as first dc plus ch 1, now and throughout**), sk next ch, * dc in next ch, ch 1, sk next ch, rep from * around, join with sl st in first dc: {117-126}{135-144-153} dc.

Rnds 2-5:

Sl st in first sp, ch 4, * dc in next sp, ch 1, rep from * around, join with sl st in first dc.

SKIRT

Rnd 1 (right side):

Fold Waistband lengthwise over drawstring so that Rnd 1 is behind Rnd 5 and ends of drawstring are threaded through Rnd 2 of adjacent sps on opposite side of Waistband, ch 1; working through both thicknesses of Rnd 5 and Rnd 1, (sc in next sp, ch 1) around, join with sl st in beg sc.

NOTE: Loop a short piece of thread around any stitch to mark Rnd 1 as right side.

Rnd 2:

Ch 3 (**counts as first dc, now and throughout**), sk next ch-1 sp and next sc, (2 dc, ch 2, 2 dc) in next ch-1 sp, sk next sc and next ch-1 sp, * dc in next sc, sk next ch-1 sp and next sc, (2 dc, ch 2, 2 dc) in next ch-1 sp, sk next sc and next ch-1 sp, rep from * around, join with sl st in first dc: {39-42}{45-48-51} ch-2 sps.

Rnds 3-6:

Ch 3, sk next 2 dc, (2 dc, ch 2, 2 dc) in next ch-2 sp, * sk next 2 dc, dc in next dc, sk next 2 dc, (2 dc, ch 2, 2 dc) in next ch-2 sp, rep from * around, join with sl st in first dc.

Rnd 7:

Ch 5, sk next 2 dc, sc in next ch-2 sp, ch 3, sk next 2 dc, * hdc in next dc, ch 3, sk next 2 dc, sc in next ch-2 sp, ch 3, sk next 2 dc, rep from * around, join with sl st in second ch of beg ch-5.

Rnd 8:

Sl st in next ch-3 sp changing to Blue (*Fig. 4, page 95*), ch 2, 2dctog in same sp, ch 2, * 3dctog in next ch-3 sp, ch 2, rep from * around, join with sl st in top of beg 2dctog changing to Green.

Rnd 9:
Ch 5, hdc in same st, * (hdc, ch 3, hdc) in next 3dctog, rep from * around, join with sl st in second ch of beg ch-5.

Rnds 10 and 11:
Rep Rnds 8 and 9.

Rnd 12:
Sl st in next ch-3 sp changing to Blue, ch 2, 2dctog in same sp, * ch 2, 3dctog in next sp, rep from * around, join with hdc in top of beg 2dctog changing to Ecru.

Rnd 13:
Ch 1, sc in last sp made, ch 3, * sc in next ch-2 sp, ch 3, rep from * around, join with sl st in beg sc. Fasten off.

FIRST MOTIF (make 1)
With Blue, ch 6, join with sl st to form ring.

Rnd 1:
Ch 1, 12 sc in ring, join with sl st in front loop of first sc *(Fig. 1, page 95)*.

Rnd 2:
Working in front loop only, ch 1, sc in first st, ch 4, (sc in next 2 sc, ch 4) 5 times, sc in last sc, join with sl st in **both** loops of beg sc: 6 ch-4 sps.

Rnd 3:
Work [(sl st, ch 2, 2 dc, ch 1, 2 dc, ch 2, sl st) in next ch-4 sp, ch 1] around, join with sl st in beg sl st, fasten off: 6 Petals.

Rnd 4:
Working **behind** Rnd 3 and in free loops of sts on Rnd 2 *(Fig. 3a, page 95)*, join Green with sl st in second sc, *† (ch 6, sc in fourth ch from hook, sl st in rem 2 chs, sl st in center of sc - Petal2 made), ch 2 †, sk next sc, sl st in next sc, rep from * 4 times **more**, then rep from † to † once, join with sl st in beg sl st. Fasten off.

Rnd 5:
With **right** side facing, join Ecru with sc in ch-1 sp of any Petal on Rnd 3 *(see Joining with Sc, page 95)*, ch 4, sc in same sp, † ch 3, sc in tip of next Petal2, ch 3, sc in ch-1 sp of next Petal on Rnd 3, ch 3, (sc, ch 4, sc) in tip of next Petal2, ch 3, sc in ch-1 sp of next Petal on Rnd 3, ch 3, sc in tip of next Petal2 †, ch 3, (sc, ch 4, sc) in ch-1 sp of next Petal on Rnd 3, rep from † to † once, join with dc in beg sc.

Rnd 6:
Ch 1, sc in last sp made, ch 3, (3 dc, ch 2, 3 dc) in next ch-4 sp, * (ch 3, sc in next ch-3 sp) 3 times, (3 dc, ch 2, 3 dc) in next ch-4 sp, ch 3, rep from * 2 times **more**, (ch 3, sc in next sp) twice, join with dc in beg sc.

Rnd 7:
Ch 1, sc in last sp made, ch 3, sc in next ch-3 sp, ch 3, (2 hdc, ch 3, 2 hdc) in next ch-2 sp, (ch 3, sc in next ch-3 sp) 4 times, ch 3, 2 hdc in next ch-2 sp, ch 1, with **right** side of Skirt facing and Rnd 13 closest to you, sl st in second ch of last ch-3 sp of Rnd 13 of **Skirt**, ch 1, 2 hdc in same sp of **Motif**, (ch 1, sl st in second ch of next ch-3 sp of Rnd 13 of **Skirt**, ch 1, sc in next ch-3 sp of **Motif**) 4 times, ch 1, sl st in second ch of next ch-3 sp of Rnd 13 of **Skirt**,

ch 1, 2 hdc in next ch-2 sp of **Motif**, ch 1, sl st in second ch of next ch-3 sp of Rnd 13 of **Skirt**, ch 1, 2 hdc in same ch-2 sp of **Motif**, (ch 3, sc in next sp) 4 times, ch 3, (2 hdc, ch 3, 2 hdc) in next ch-2 sp, (ch 3, sc in next sp) twice, ch 3, join with sl st in beg sc. Fasten off.

MIDDLE MOTIF
(make {11-12}{13-14-15})
Rnds 1-6:
Work same as Rnds 1-6 of First Motif.

Rnd 7:
Placing new Motif to the left of previous Motif, ch 1, sc in last sp made, ch 3, sc in next sp, ch 3, 2 hdc in next ch-2 sp, ch 1, sl st in second ch of corresponding ch-3 sp at lower left corner of **previous Motif**, ch 1, 2 hdc in same ch-2 sp of **new Motif**, (ch 1, sl st in second ch of next ch-3 sp of **previous Motif**, ch 1, sc in next ch-3 sp of **new Motif**) 4 times, ch 1, sl st in second ch of next ch-3 sp of **previous Motif**, ch 1, 2 hdc in next ch-2 sp of **new Motif**, ch 1, sl st in same st of Rnd 13 of **Skirt** as last joining sl st made, ch 1, 2 hdc in same sp of **new Motif**, (ch 1, sl st in second ch of next ch-3 sp of Rnd 13 of **Skirt**, ch 1, sc in next ch-3 sp of **new Motif**) 4 times, ch 1, sl st in second ch of next ch-3 sp of Rnd 13 of **Skirt**, ch 1, 2 hdc in next ch-2 sp of **new Motif**, ch 1, sl st in second ch of next ch-3 sp of Rnd 13 of **Skirt**, ch 1, 2 hdc in same ch-2 sp of **new Motif**, (ch 3, sc in next sp) 4 times, ch 3, (2 hdc, ch 3, 2 hdc) in next ch-2 sp, (ch 3, sc in next sp) twice, ch 3, join with sl st in beg sc. Fasten off.

LAST MOTIF (make 1)
Rnds 1-6:
Follow instructions for Rnds 1-6 of First Motif.

Rnd 7:
Placing new Motif to the left of previous Motif, ch 1, sc in last sp made, ch 3, sc in next sp, ch 3, 2 hdc in next ch-2 sp, ch 1, sl st in second ch of corresponding ch-3 sp at lower left corner of **previous Motif**, ch 1, 2 hdc in same ch-2 sp of **new Motif**, (ch 1, sl st in second ch of next ch-3 sp of **previous Motif**, ch 1, sc in next ch-3 sp of **new Motif**) 4 times, ch 1, sl st in second ch of next ch-3 sp of **previous Motif**, ch 1, 2 hdc in next ch-2 sp of **new Motif**, ch 1, sl st in same st of Rnd 13 of **Skirt** as last joining sl st made, ch 1, 2 hdc in same sp of **new Motif**, (ch 1, sl st in second ch of next ch-3 sp of Rnd 13 of **Skirt**, ch 1, sc in next ch-3 sp of **new Motif**) 4 times, ch 1, sl st in second ch of next ch-3 sp of Rnd 13 of **Skirt**, ch 1, 2 hdc in next ch-2 sp of **new Motif**, ch 1, sl st in same st of Rnd 13 of **Skirt** as first joining st made, ch 1, 2 hdc in same ch-2 sp of **new Motif**, (ch 1, sl st in second ch of next ch-3 sp of **First Motif**, ch 1, sc in next ch-3 sp of **new Motif**) 4 times, ch 1, sl st in second ch of next ch-3 sp of **First Motif**, ch 1, 2 hdc in next ch-2 sp of **new Motif**, ch 1, sl st in second ch of next ch-3 sp of **First Motif**, ch 1, 2 hdc in same ch-2 sp of **new Motif**, (ch 3, sc in next ch-3 sp of **new Motif**) twice, ch 3, join with sl st in beg sc. Fasten off.

SKIRT SECTION 2

Rnd 1:
With **right** side facing, join Blue with sc in joining between First and Last Motifs, *† [ch 1, (dc, ch 1) 3 times in second ch of next ch-3 sp, sc in second ch of next ch-3 sp] twice, ch 1, (dc, ch 1) 3 times in second ch of next ch-3 sp †, sc in joining between next 2 Motifs, rep from * {11-12}{13-14-15} times **more**, then rep from † to † once, join with sl st in beg sc.

Rnd 2:
Ch 2, dc in next dc, ch 3, sc in next dc, ch 3, * [(sk next ch, YO, pull up a loop in **next** st, YO, pull through 2 loops on hook) 3 times, YO, pull through all loops on hook–3dctog made], ch 3, sc in next dc, ch 3, rep from * around to last dc, dc in last dc, join with sl st in beg dc changing to Green.

Rnd 3:
Ch 1, sc in same st, ch 1, sk next ch-3 sp, (dc, ch 1) 3 times in next sc, sk next ch-3 sp, * sc in next 3dctog, ch 1, sk next ch-3 sp, (dc, ch 1) 3 times in next sc, sk next ch-3 sp, rep from * around, join with sl st in beg sc.

Rnd 4:
Rep Rnd 2, changing to Blue.

Rnd 5:
Rep Rnd 3.

Rnd 6:
Rep Rnd 2, changing to Ecru.

Rnd 7:
Rep Rnd 3.

Rnd 8:
Rep Rnd 2, do **not** change colors.

Rnd 9:
Ch 1, sc in same st, ch 3, sc in next sp, ch 3, sc in next sc, ch 3, sc in next sp, * ch 3, sc in next 3dctog, ch 3, sc in next sp, ch 3, sc in next sc, ch 3, sc in next sp, rep from * around, join with dc in beg sc: {156-168} {180-192-204} ch-3 sps.

Rnd 10:
Ch 1, sc in last sp made, ch 3, (sc in next sp, ch 3) around, join with sl st in beg sc.

Rnd 11:
Sk first sc, sl st in next sp, ch 3, (2 dc, ch 2, 2 dc) in next sp, * dc in next sp, (2 dc, ch 2, 2 dc) in next sp, rep from * around, join with sl st in first dc.

Rnds 12-31:
Ch 3, sk next 2 dc, (2 dc, ch 2, 2 dc) in next ch-2 sp, * sk next 2 dc, dc in next dc, sk next 2 dc, (2 dc, ch 2, 2 dc) in next ch-2 sp, rep from * around, join with sl st in first dc.

Rnd 32:
Ch 3, sk next 2 dc, (2 dc, ch 2, 2 dc) in next ch-2 sp, sk next 2 dc, dc in next dc, *† sk next dc, dc in next dc, (2 dc, ch 2, 2 dc) in next ch-2 sp, dc in next dc, sk next dc, dc in next dc †, [sk next 2 dc, (2 dc, ch 2, 2 dc) in next ch-2 sp, sk next 2 dc, dc in next dc] twice, rep from * {24-26} {28-30-32} times **more**, then rep from † to † once, sk next 2 dc, (2 dc, ch 2, 2 dc) in next ch-2 sp, join with sl st in first dc.

Rnd 33:
Ch 3, sk next 2 dc, (2 dc, ch 2, 2 dc) in next ch-2 sp, sk next 2 dc, dc in next dc, *† sk next 2 dc, dc in next dc, (2 dc, ch 2, 2 dc) in next ch-2 sp, dc in next dc, sk next 2 dc, dc in next

dc †, [sk next 2 dc, (2 dc, ch 2, 2 dc) in next ch-2 sp), sk next 2 dc, dc in next dc] twice, rep from * {24-26} {28-30-32} times **more**, then rep from † to † once, sk next 2 dc, (2 dc, ch 2, 2 dc) in next ch-2 sp, join with sl st in first dc.

Rnd 34:

Ch 3, sk next 2 dc, (2 dc, ch 2, 2 dc) in next ch-2 sp, sk next 2 dc, dc in next dc, *† sk next dc, dc in next 2 dc, (2 dc, ch 2, 2 dc) in next ch-2 sp, dc in next 2 dc, sk next dc, dc in next dc †, [sk next 2 dc, (2 dc, ch 2, 2 dc) in next ch-2 sp), sk next 2 dc, dc in next dc] twice, rep from * {24-26} {28-30-32} times **more**, then rep from † to † once, sk next 2 dc, (2 dc, ch 2, 2 dc) in next ch-2 sp, join with sl st in first dc.

Rnd 35:

Ch 3, sk next 2 dc, (2 dc, ch 2, 2 dc) in next ch-2 sp, sk next 2 dc, dc in next dc, *† sk next 2 dc, dc in next 2 dc, (2 dc, ch 2, 2 dc) in next ch-2 sp, dc in next 2 dc, sk next 2 dc, dc in next dc †, [sk next 2 dc, (2 dc, ch 2, 2 dc) in next ch-2 sp), sk next 2 dc, dc in next dc] twice, rep from * {24-26}{28-30-32} times **more**, then rep from † to † once, sk next 2 dc, (2 dc, ch 2, 2 dc) in next ch-2 sp, join with sl st in first dc.

Rnd 36:

Ch 3, sk next 2 dc, (2 dc, ch 2, 2 dc) in next ch-2 sp, sk next 2 dc, dc in next dc, *† sk next dc, dc in next 3 dc, (2 dc, ch 2, 2 dc) in next ch-2 sp, dc in next 3 dc, sk next dc, dc in next dc †, [sk next 2 dc, (2 dc, ch 2, 2 dc) in next ch-2 sp), sk next 2 dc, dc in next dc] twice, rep from * {24-26} {28-30-32} times **more**, then rep from † to † once, sk next 2 dc, (2 dc, ch 2, 2 dc) in next ch-2 sp, join with sl st in first dc.

Rnd 37:

Ch 3, sk next 2 dc, (2 dc, ch 2, 2 dc) in next ch-2 sp, sk next 2 dc, dc in next dc, *† sk next 2 dc, dc in next 3 dc, (2 dc, ch 2, 2 dc) in next ch-2 sp, dc in next 3 dc, sk next 2 dc, dc in next dc †, [sk next 2 dc, (2 dc, ch 2, 2 dc) in next ch-2 sp), sk next 2 dc, dc in next dc] twice, rep from * {24-26}{28-30-32} times **more**, then rep from † to † once, sk next 2 dc, (2 dc, ch 2, 2 dc) in next ch-2 sp, join with sl st in first dc.

Rnd 38:

Ch 3, sk next 2 dc, (2 dc, ch 2, 2 dc) in next ch-2 sp, sk next 2 dc, dc in next dc, *† sk next dc, dc in next 4 dc, (2 dc, ch 2, 2 dc) in next ch-2 sp, dc in next 4 dc, sk next dc, dc in next dc †, [sk next 2 dc, (2 dc, ch 2, 2 dc) in next ch-2 sp), sk next 2 dc, dc in next dc] twice, rep from * {24-26}{28-30-32} times **more**, then

rep from † to † once, sk next 2 dc, (2 dc, ch 2, 2 dc) in next ch-2 sp, join with sl st in first dc.

Rnd 39:

Ch 3, sk next 2 dc, (2 dc, ch 2, hdc in top of dc just made, 2 dc) in next ch-2 sp, sk next 2 dc, dc in next dc, *† sk next 2 dc, dc in next 4 dc, (2 dc, ch 2, hdc in top of dc just made, 2 dc) in next ch-2 sp, dc in next 4 dc, sk next 2 dc, dc in next dc †, [sk next 2 dc, (2 dc, ch 2, hdc in top of dc just made, 2 dc) in next ch-2 sp), sk next 2 dc, dc in next dc] twice, rep from * {24-26}{28-30-32} times **more**, then rep from † to † once, sk next 2 dc, (2 dc, ch 2, hdc in top of dc just made, 2 dc) in next ch-2 sp, join with sl st in first dc. Fasten off.

General instructions

ABBREVIATIONS

approx	approximately	mm	millimeters	
beg	beginning	rem	remaining	
BP	back post	rep	repeat	
BPdc	Back Post double crochet(s)	Rnd(s)	Round(s)	
ch(s)	chain(s)	sc	single crochet(s)	
cm	centimeters	sk	skip	
dc	double crochet(s)	sl st	slip stitch	
dec	decrease	sp(s)	space(s)	
FP	front post	st(s)	stitch(es)	
FPdc	Front Post double crochet(s)	tog	together	
hdc	half double crochet(s)	tr	treble crochet(s)	
inc	increase	YO	yarn over	

* — work instructions following * as many **more** times as indicated in addition to the first time.

† to † — work all instructions from first † to second † as **many** times as specified.

( ) or [ ] — work enclosed instructions as **many** times as specified by the number immediately following **or** work all enclosed instructions in the stitch or space indicated **or** contains explanatory remarks.

colon (:) — the number(s) given after a colon at the end of a row or round denote(s) the number of stitches you should have on that row or round.

GAUGE

Exact gauge is **essential** for proper fit. Before beginning your project, make a sample swatch in the thread and hook specified. After completing the swatch, measure it, counting your stitches and rows or rounds carefully. If your swatch is larger or smaller than specified, **make another, changing hook size to get the correct gauge**. Keep trying until you find the size hook that will give you the specified gauge. Once proper gauge is obtained, measure width of garment approximately every 3" (7.5 cm) to be sure gauge remains consistent.

CROCHET TERMINOLOGY		
UNITED STATES		**INTERNATIONAL**
slip stitch (slip st)	=	single crochet (sc)
single crochet (sc)	=	double crochet (dc)
half double crochet (hdc)	=	half treble crochet (htr)
double crochet (dc)	=	treble crochet (tr)
treble crochet (tr)	=	double treble crochet (dtr)
double treble crochet (dtr)	=	triple treble crochet (ttr)
triple treble crochet (tr tr)	=	quadruple treble crochet (qtr)
skip	=	miss

STEEL CROCHET HOOKS																
U.S.	00	0	1	2	3	4	5	6	7	8	9	10	11	12	13	14
Metric - mm	3.5	3.25	2.75	2.25	2.1	2	1.9	1.8	1.65	1.5	1.4	1.3	1.1	1	.85	.75

◼◻◻◻ BEGINNER	Projects for first-time crocheters using basic stitches. Minimal shaping.
◼◼◻◻ EASY	Projects using yarn with basic stitches, repetitive stitch patterns, simple color changes, and simple shaping and finishing.
◼◼◼◻ INTERMEDIATE	Projects using a variety of techniques, such as basic lace patterns or color patterns, mid-level shaping and finishing.
◼◼◼◼ EXPERIENCED	Projects with intricate stitch patterns, techniques and dimension, such as non-repeating patterns, multi-color techniques, fine threads, small hooks, detailed shaping and refined finishing.

HINTS

Good finishing techniques make a big difference in the quality of the piece. Make a habit of taking care of loose ends as you work. Thread a tapestry needle with the end. With **wrong** side facing, weave the needle through several stitches, then reverse the direction and weave it back through several stitches. When ends are secure, clip them off close to the work.

WASHING AND BLOCKING

For a more professional look, pieces should be washed and blocked. Using a mild detergent and warm water and being careful not to rub, twist, or wring, gently squeeze suds through the piece. Rinse several times in cool, clear water. Roll piece in a clean terry towel and gently press out the excess moisture. Lay piece on a flat surface and shape to proper size; where needed, pin in place using rust-proof pins. Allow to dry completely.

JOINING WITH SC

When instructed to join with sc, begin with a slip knot on hook. Insert hook in stitch or space indicated, YO and pull up a loop, YO and draw through both loops on hook.

ZEROS

To consolidate the length of an involved pattern, zeros are used so that all sizes can be combined. For example, repeat Rows 1 and 2 {0-1}{1-2-2} time(s) means the first size would do nothing, the next two sizes would repeat the rows once, and the largest sizes would repeat the rows twice.

FRONT LOOP ONLY

Work only in loop(s) indicated by arrow *(Fig. 1)*.

Fig. 1

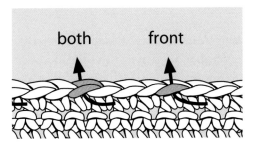

POST STITCH

Work around post of stitch indicated, inserting hook in direction of arrow *(Fig. 2)*.

Fig. 2

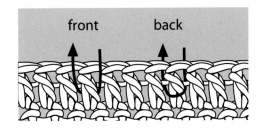

FREE LOOPS

After working in Back or Front Loops Only on a row or round, there will be a ridge of unused loops. These are called the free loops. Later, when instructed to work in the free loops of the same row or round, work in these loops *(Fig. 3a)*.
When instructed to work in free loops of a chain, work in loop indicated by arrow *(Fig. 3b)*.

Fig. 3a   **Fig. 3b**

 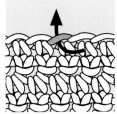

CHANGING COLORS

Work the last stitch to within one step of completion, hook new color *(Fig. 4)* and draw through all loops on hook.

Fig. 4

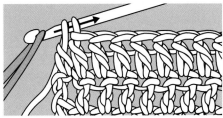

WORKING IN TOP OF OR IN CENTER OF STITCH JUST MADE

When instructed to work in top of **or** in center of stitch just made, work the stitch by inserting the hook through one horizontal bar and one vertical bar of specified stitch *(Fig. 5)* and complete stitch as instructed.

Fig. 5

Thread information

Each piece in this leaflet was made using Aunt Lydia's® Classic Crochet Cotton Thread (size 10). Any brand of size 10 cotton thread may be used. Remember, to arrive at the finished size, it is the GAUGE/TENSION that is important, not the brand of thread.

For your convenience, listed below are the colors used to create our photography models.

MIDNIGHT IN THE GARDEN JACKET
Black - #12 Black
Red - #492 Burgundy
Yellow - #421 Goldenrod

MIDNIGHT IN THE GARDEN SKIRT
Black - #12 Black
Red - #492 Burgundy
Yellow - #421 Goldenrod

DANCER'S DELIGHT TOP
#226 Natural

DANCER'S DELIGHT SKIRT
#226 Natural

GARDEN OF DREAMS TOP
#154 Cream

GARDEN OF DREAMS SKIRT
#154 Cream

YESTERDAY ONCE MORE TOP
#1056 Chambray

YESTERDAY ONCE MORE SKIRT
Ecru - #21 Linen
Blue - #1056 Chambray
Green - #661 Frosty Green